THE MILE END ROAD PROMENADE.—*Page* 101.

EAST LONDON

SKETCHES OF CHRISTIAN WORK
AND WORKERS

HENRY WALKER

THE RELIGIOUS TRACT SOCIETY

56 PATERNOSTER ROW AND 65 ST. PAUL'S CHURCHYARD

First published by the Religious Tract Society, 1896.

Reprinted by:
Peter Marcan Publications, 1987.
31, Rowliff Rd, High Wycombe, Bucks HP12 3LD,
England, U.K.

East End Reprint Series Number 1
ISBN: 0 9504211 8 9

Number 2: *Down in the East End* – an illustrated
anthology of descriptive and imaginative prose extracts
from the late nineteenth century to the present day.
ISBN: 0 9510289 2 8

Number 3: *One Dinner A Week, and, Travels in the East.*
Illustrated account of conditions in Limehouse, first
published in 1884 by the London Cottage Mission.
ISBN 0 9510289 7 9

Number 4: *A Mid-Victorian East End Album* – a
collection of illustrations and articles from The
Illustrated London News, The Illustrated Times, The
Builder, and Building News, 1843–1873 relating to
architecture, new building projects and life in Tower
Hamlets, Hackney, and Newham.
ISBN: 0 9510289 6 0

Printed and bound by Short Run Press Ltd, Exeter

PREFACE

—◆—

THESE chapters are the record of a series of visits in the years 1894–95 to the districts they describe. The pictures given of life as it is lived to-day in London's vast Eastern Hemisphere are accompanied with some account of the newer problems which now confront the Christian social worker, and also of the newer resources and methods which have been developed in order to meet them. The contrast which the writer is able to make between the East London of forty years since and that of to-day may be as new to the present generation as it is startling to himself. May the evidences of great social and religious progress which he has brought together help to lighten the burden and animate the spirits of present-day workers in this consecrated seed-field in their times of difficulty and discouragement! Happily, the workers of to-day have still among them those of both sexes whose names are an inspiration to fellow-labourers in all lands where the English language is spoken. May these brief memoirs, notwithstanding their inevitable omissions and short-comings, be taken as a tribute and a 'God-speed' to all those East London yokefellows whom the writer has been privileged to meet with in his visits, as well as to those whom having not seen he yet knows in the spirit!

H. W.

CONTENTS

LIST OF ILLUSTRATIONS

EAST LONDON

——◆——

I

SUNDAY IN EAST LONDON

TUPENDOUS as are its burdens and its problems, never did the great world which we call East London present such inspiring aspects or so fascinate the social and religious worker as it does to-day. Who shall describe even the surface of the vast panorama of the East London of to-day! In picturesqueness of roof and sky-line, this great congeries of towns, with a population of 1,600,000 persons, startles and pleases the world-tourist's eye. Its great imperial highways, its newer public buildings, its vast and ever-increasing mileage of lofty industrial dwellings, and the human tides which surge along its streets, are beginning to be discovered by Londoners themselves. It is in Aldgate and Whitechapel, not in the magnificent and luxurious West, and amid the overwhelming and concentrated traffic of commercial London beyond the old Eastern city gate, and not in the Old Court suburb, that the spectator is nearer to the heart of London life. Here and farther East he feels the buoyancy of the rising tide and the energy of the younger life. New and imposing buildings, educational, religious, and charitable, everywhere meet the eye. The great and almost illimitable plain of East London is thickly set with towers and spires and hospitable beacons stretching still farther and farther East to the far Essex horizon beyond. They rise like great friendly lighthouses from the once dreary social swamp or the cheerless highway, telling of newer forces and helpful centres now available for a hardly-pressed people.

Close by the greatest hospital in the kingdom, the London Hospital, there now rises the greatest elementary school for poor children of which England can boast—the Jews' Free School in Spitalfields. Here, too, are found old beacons of the historic past, noble parish churches, bearing up bravely amid almost overwhelming cares, and in friendly touch with almost magnificent mission halls, of which the West End might be proud.

Not far from the People's Palace, the Universities of Oxford and Cambridge stretch out a helping hand to East London. Beautiful and capacious college settlements have arisen in Whitechapel and Bethnal Green, and a still newer centre in Canning Town. At Shoreditch and Mile End are two Nonconformist temples, each led by one of the foremost of London preachers, the congregations in which are counted by thousands—centres of religious life which are among the most auspicious pledges for the East London of the future.

If, as seems undeniable, East London has in recent years become the scene of social and religious movements which are largely changing the face of society, the Sunday aspect of the place should afford some clues to the still more hopeful future which seems to be in store.

Sunday religious agencies, although by no means the only forms of activity in the district, are the chief expression of the regenerative forces which are at work. It is on Sundays that the newer as well as the older forms of propaganda find their chief opportunity.

Some of the greatest problems of modern times have recently taken on new aspects, and are probably working themselves out to unforeseen and eventful issues. For the East London of today, although still largely consisting, as is supposed, of the most destitute population in the kingdom, is no longer the inert, inorganic, unaspiring, unquickened world of a quarter of a century since, almost narcotised with unvarying labour. Since that period it has been vivified from many sources, both within and without. Immense and unwieldy as it may be, East London is largely acquiring a social and organising life of its own. It is no longer swallowed up in its own vastness.

In spite of enormous difficulties, the older methods and equipment for church work in East London still survive in the more historic. centres, although under greatly changed conditions. Magnificently built churches are still the nucleus of parochial work. On the other hand, some phases of religious organisation and church life would seem to have passed away, at least for a time. The list of places of worship which have been given up and devoted to non-religious purposes during the last twenty-five years is a long one. Their activities and ministrations in the district may have taken other forms, but some of them will be sadly missed in a Sunday visit to East London.

But the greatest and most portentous of the newer religious and social phenomena of East London, more especially in their Sunday aspects, has now to be mentioned. It is the startling and overshadowing growth of Anglo-Judaism. The extraordinary increase in the numbers of the Jewish population, their progressive consolidation and irresistible expansion, and their unceasing overflow still farther East are by far the most important and significant of the influences which are transforming great parishes in East London.[1]

For reasons which will be mentioned, it is impossible to assign any limits to the growth and extension of this Anglo-Jewish population and its effects on the future of East London. The aspects of the Sunday are necessarily greatly affected by it. And yet, as will be seen, the Jewish Sunday agencies in use for religious and educational purposes are on a great scale, and of no little interest and import. On the purely educational side, the scheme for a Jewish Toynbee Hall at Mile End will still further colour the character of the Sunday in the district. Altogether, the contribution of Judaism to the Sunday and week-day life of

---

[1] In two parishes alone—Whitechapel and Mile End—the Jewish population already amounts to at least 35,000. In the words of Lord Rothschild, uttered at a recent meeting of the Jewish Board of Guardians, ' We have now a new Poland on our hands in East London. Our first business is to humanise our Jewish immigrants, and then to Anglicise them.'

the East End is, perhaps, the most important factor to be reckoned with in future religious work for East London.

The great University Missions and Settlements also necessarily come under notice in these papers. In Whitechapel and Bethnal Green, the Universities of Oxford and Cambridge have planted vigorous offshoots from the parent stock, and with great courage and perseverance they have commenced the experiment of settling colonies of their own laymen to live among the inhabitants of the East End, and there, in the evening and other periods of leisure, to carry on educational and religious work, or both, amongst their less happily circumstanced fellow-residents in the East. At Oxford House and at Mansfield House these missions have a more distinctively religious character. They will be found contributing in their own way to the religious character of the Sunday as well as to week-day evangelising agencies.

By no means the least important of the newer agencies is the mission founded by the Society of Friends. At the Bedford Institute, Spitalfields (the famous historical site associated with the Quakerism of two hundred years since), and at other permanent buildings recently erected in the great East London parishes, a highly interesting and expansive work is in progress, on the lines of the 'forward movement' lately adopted by the newer generation of Quakers, for the education and spiritual welfare of the poorer and more neglected classes. Here again the Sunday and week-day work is of great interest. It marks the definite adoption by the newer generation of Friends of mission work with an evangelistic object as a new development of Quakerism. The result so far is a valuable and highly promising contribution to the great army of evangelical lay workers.

The Tower Hamlets Mission has an eventful and inspiring record in the annals of East London evangelistic effort. Both at its headquarters, the Great Assembly Hall of Mile End, and by means of its many outdoor services, it is still carrying on its important and beneficent work.

During the last decade the ever-widening field has engaged the attention and devoted labours of the Wesleyan East End Mission. Not a few of the most zealous and gifted of Wesleyan evangelists have maintained here an arduous campaign, especially in districts of the most evil repute.

Less distinctly religious, but for the most part marking a social movement which is as yet in its infancy, are the Sunday afternoon meetings, lectures, and discussions on religious and miscellaneous topics. Those which are known as Pleasant Sunday Afternoons have already taken root in the East of London. Largely countenanced by the clergy and Nonconformist ministers, they are generally held in connection with places of worship.

On the other hand, the non-religious Sunday meetings promoted by the Labour organisations, held in Town Halls and other non-ecclesiastical buildings, have equally become a regular part of the East London Sunday programme; they are being watched with eager and sometimes anxious eyes, for they are very gradually but surely becoming a social force in East End circles. The part which the clergy take in these gatherings, at the invitation of the men, promises to be of great value in the mutual relations of the Church and the Labour classes.

In these attempts to sketch the Sunday aspects of East London the background of the past will not be forgotten. Not a few of the newer workers draw helpful inspiration from the example of men and women of unrecorded lives, from whose hands they received the living torch. The rank and file of the great army of East End workers remain unnamed, like the preacher of Matthew Arnold's beautiful poem; but the thought of those who have gone before is still a consecrating force in the hearts of their successors.

> ' 'Twas August, and the fierce sun overhead
>   Smote on the squalid streets of Bethnal Green,
>   And the pale weaver, through his windows seen
> In Spitalfields, looked thrice dispirited.
> I met a preacher there I knew, and said:
>   "Ill and o'erworked, how fare you in this scene?"
>   "Bravely!" said he; "for I of late have been
> Much cheered with thoughts of Christ, the Living Bread."
>
> O human soul! as long as thou canst so
>   Set up a mark of everlasting light,
> Above the howling senses' ebb and flow,
> To cheer thee, and to right thee if thou roam,
>   Not with lost toil thou labourest through the night!
> Thou mak'st the heaven thou hop'st indeed thy home.'

II

WHITECHAPEL

THE Aldgate entrance to the great continent which we call East London is a welcome surprise to the stranger. Passing the boundary of the old city wall, we are at once in the heart of the most spacious, most picturesque, and most impressive of the great streets of the metropolis. 'Of all the roads which lead into London and out of it,' says our chief contemporary historiographer of the 'East End,' 'this of Whitechapel is the broadest and noblest by nature.' On Sunday the closing of the shops adds to the dignity of the thoroughfare. Moreover, there is an air of historic London all around us. Gabled houses of the time of De Foe, of Thomas Cromwell, of Strype, and other residents in old Whitechapel ; and old inns, with the relics of galleried yards of the stage-coach period of history, are suggestive of bygone times, and of the memorable events of which this great Essex road has been the scene.

On a fine summer Sunday morning let us walk down this noble and spacious Whitechapel boulevard, the chief and indeed almost the only open-air resort in the district for some eighty thousand people entirely devoid of park and recreation ground.

The stranger to the scene is at first baffled and bewildered. The roadway is filled with large tramcars, and the footways are crowded with groups of busy loungers. But we soon begin to make the great and startling discovery which awaits every new-comer into Whitechapel. Here, in spite of the English-looking surroundings, he is practically in a foreign land, so far as

The Whitechapel Boulevard.

language and race are concerned. The people are neither French
nor English, Germans nor Americans, but Jews. In this Whitechapel Ghetto the English visitor almost feels himself one of a

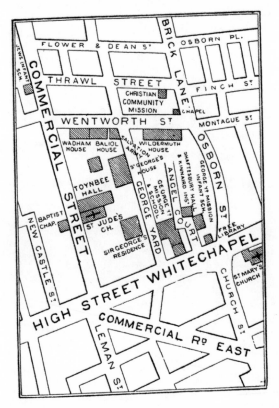

subject race in the presence of dominant and overwhelming
invaders. Yet the crowds are peaceful and entirely non-aggres-
sive in demeanour. There is no sign of lawlessness, or of
molestation of the minority. Indeed, in this respect White-

chapel on Sunday, as on other days, compares most favourably with many parts of Gentile London.

The wide street continues to be crowded, although the church-bells have ceased. St. Mary's, the fine parish church, has gathered its congregation of some six or seven hundred. The Board schools are filling with Jewish children attending the Hebrew religion-classes.

At St. Jude's, in the heart of the Ghetto, the choir sometimes

HIGH STREET, WHITECHAPEL

outnumber the congregation; and at Toynbee Hall, close by, where Sunday morning science classes are open for students, some scores of young men are entering with their text-books. But turning again to the great High Street and its hurrying thousands, you would say that, in the main, Whitechapel spends its Sundays out of doors.

Reserving for a time any detailed notice of the Christian agencies at work in Whitechapel, it will be well to give pre-

cedence to the Jewish population and the remarkable character
which the Sunday is acquiring for what are known as 'communal' purposes in Jewish quarters. The synagogues, the
chevras, and the Jewish Sunday schools are the three great
institutions which lie in the foreground of the view. Strange as
it may sound to Christian ears, Sunday, although not a day of
obligation in Judaism, is, at least in the East of London, a day
of considerable religious activity. In some respects, as will be
seen again and again in these investigations, the Sunday religious
gatherings of the Jews would appear to be of as great importance
to the rising generation as the synagogue service of the preced-
ing Sabbath.

Whitechapel abounds with synagogues great and small, with
chevras, and with Sunday schools for Jewish children. The
synagogues (the fact may be new to many of our readers) are
by no means wholly disused for religious purposes on the
Sunday. Every synagogue in East London is in fact open
every Sunday, as on other days, for morning and evening service,
the usual hours in summer being 7 A.M. and 7 P.M., and in winter
3.30 or 4 P.M. 'Sunday afternoon and evening,' writes a well-
known London rabbi, 'are of enormous service in the communal
life of the Jews, the word "communal" covering all movements
having the intellectual, moral, and spiritual welfare of the
community as their aim. Moreover, all meetings for religious,
educational, and charitable purposes are preferably held on
Sundays.'

The synagogues may not figure largely in the street scenery
of Whitechapel, or attract the attention of the wayfarer by the
sound of the church-going bell, as do the beautiful peals from
the towers and steeples of the Christian temples around. The
visitor may, in fact, pass without knowing it the Aldgate side-
street where stands the 'Hebrew Cathedral' of London, the
Great Synagogue, where the office of senior warden has been
filled by the Rothschild family for three generations, and where
the founder of the family is buried. A little to the north, in
Bevis Marks, is the Spanish and Portuguese synagogue. Between
Crosby Place and St. Helen's Square is the New Synagogue.

It is not a little significant of the great influx of foreign Jews, and the multiplication of those already domiciled in White- chapel, that within the last four or five years synagogues have been built and opened within a short distance of each other in the New Road, Vine Court, Greenfield Street, and Great Alie Street. Among the lesser synagogues are those

A SUNDAY MORNING GROUP.

in Scarborough Street and Mansell Street, Commercial Road, and Plummer's Row.

A still more notable sign of a rapidly increasing population

JEWISH GIRLS COMING OUT OF SCHOOL.

and the problems which it brings in its train is the project for a new and very large synagogue in the Commercial Road, for the purpose of relieving the more congested districts of White-chapel. It is to be called the New Hambro' Synagogue, the old site having been abandoned in favour of the less populous area farther east. The rebuilt Hambro' Synagogue is to seat 1000 male worshippers and 400 female worshippers, twice the number at any existing constituent synagogue, at the cost of some £30,000.

Religious services for children are not seldom held in the East End synagogues; but it is not here that we shall see how largely Sunday is devoted by the Jews to the education and nurture of their children, under the ardent supervision of the leaders of the community.

The Jewish Sunday schools are a great and impressive feature of the Whitechapel and East London Sunday. The religious education of the children, as arranged by the great leaders of London Judaism, is of the first importance, and extraordinary efforts and sacrifices are made to promote it. The distinctively Jewish buildings of so poor a district as Whitechapel are quite unequal to the needs of the closely-packed population, and the immense overflow of children has had to be provided for from other sources. Accordingly the capacious new school-buildings of the London School Board have during the last few years been readily offered and eagerly accepted for the Sunday use of Jewish children. The result is that almost all the Board schools in Whitechapel, Spitalfields, Mile End, and Stepney are appropriated to Jewish children on the Sunday. At the present time there is no Board school in any district of East London, where Jews reside in considerable numbers, which is not used on Sunday for this purpose. Any properly accredited applica-tion—and these are increasing every year—suffices to obtain at once the necessary permission.

A visit from a stranger never fails to excite his astonishment at the number of children in attendance. At Whitechapel, the large Board schools in Settle Street, Old Castle Street, and Berner Street, Commercial Road, stand, perhaps, at the head of the list as regards children attending for instruction in the Scriptures and knowledge of Hebrew. At Old Castle Street school the number of Jewish children attending religious classes on the Sunday is often one thousand. Many other illustrations could be given, showing the concern for the education of the young which distinguishes the Jewish community as a whole, under the inspiration and organisation of the Central or Federated Synagogues, and in accordance with the whole bent of modern Anglo-Judaism.

Such, then, is the brighter and better side of the Jewish Sunday in Whitechapel, and indeed, as we shall see hereafter, in the other Jewish quarters of East London—in Spitalfields, Mile End, and Stepney. But if our Sunday visit should take us away from the great main thoroughfare, which wears its holiday aspect on Sunday, and we should turn into the side-streets, into the actual Ghetto, a far different picture presents itself. We shall be appalled at the sight, which can only be paralleled by the Jewish quarter of some Polish or Galician town. We are among the poorest and densest population of the British Isles, packed together in a state of inhuman, solid, and sodden poverty. The population of Whitechapel, which averages eight hundred to the acre, here rises to three thousand. The scenes and the problems which result from the Continental Jews' lower standard of life and subsistence have been sufficiently described in Mr. Charles Booth's recent work on *Life and Labour in East London*. The practical impossibility of changing the habits of the adult population is keenly felt by the leaders of London Judaism, and hence the extraordinary efforts made for educating and Anglicising the children, which are so great a feature in East London both on Sundays and throughout the week.

The great lesson of Sunday in Whitechapel, as far as the Jews are concerned, has to be told. In this single parish are congregated some sixteen thousand poor Jews. Twenty thousand more are easily included within the half-mile radius. Yet, strange as it may seem, this great and largely squalid colony is a peaceful and law-abiding population. On the larger scale it

S.^T MARY'S, WHITECHAPEL

may even be said to be a moral population. Drunkenness is almost unknown; temperance societies are unheard of, for the Jew is never intoxicated. The public-houses will be full on Saturday and Sunday night, but not a Jewish face will be seen there. Personal violence towards women is almost unknown. Licentiousness among women is equally rare. Family ties are sacred. Considering that Whitechapel is overwhelmingly a colony of aliens, the consequences, socially and politically, might have been serious; a disaffected people might have been a standing menace to London. Whitechapel might have become a Belleville. Happily, it is not the home of malcontent refugees or political anarchists. Nothing, in fact, is more remarkable on Sunday than the quiet and orderliness of a great population of aliens in faith and speech, who, from their point of view, are under no obligation religiously to observe the day, and who are, it must be said, less aggressive in the streets than many of their better circumstanced co-residents.

Such are some of the Sunday aspects of the East London Jewry. The great Jewish problem will confront us again and again in these inquiries, and it may be that the religious and educational activities of Judaism which we have so briefly noticed will probably assume increasing importance as we trace their widening area in the great parishes contiguous to Whitechapel.

Leaving the Jews' quarter, we turn to an entirely different scene. On the opposite side of the High Street stands a gracious beacon, the historic church of St. Mary's, Whitechapel, with its noble spire, its open-air pulpit, and its beautiful church-garden. Even as a street scene it is a beautiful sight; it stands for a sweeter air, a higher and more humane civilisation than that which we have left behind us. St. Mary's, moreover, is rich in hallowed associations and cherished names. It has for generations been the centre and fortress of East End Evangelical pastors and preachers. Its rectors during this time have been men of note, conspicuous as preachers, parish workers, and organisers. The names of Weldon Champneys, Cohen, Kitto, and Robinson still stir the memory of Whitechapel citizens.

The work which these able and devoted men were able to achieve, and the inspiring examples they have bequeathed to their successors, are gratefully portrayed in some of the most beautiful of the sculptures and stained-glass memorials which adorn the parish church.

The church of St. Mary Matfelon—to give it the old historic name—is itself a message of beauty and graciousness in such a quarter. Its noble spire rises two hundred feet in height, far above the houses of the populous and struggling district around, a striking and commanding feature visible far and wide. The beautifully-toned bells are filling the air with their inviting peal. Through the crowded streets of loungers, well-to-do church-goers of the middle classes are wending their way to morning service. We enter with them, and find ourselves in a large, spacious, impressive, and richly-decorated building. The church, it should be said, is the grateful and lavish gift of a former parishioner : the lofty roof, richly-coloured walls, and the sculptures and stained-glass windows betoken alike the costliness of the offering and the giver's conception of a great church for East London. As St. Mary's, Whitechapel, is one of the foremost in popularity and equipment for parish work, and one of the best attended of the great East End churches, everything that may account for its reputation will well deserve attention.

The church seats thirteen hundred people. The services are fully choral ; the Psalms are chanted both morning and evening, the congregation being led by the surpliced choir. The musical service, though keeping pace with the increasing capacities of present-day congregations, is always well within congregational lines. The growing delight in singing as an act of common worship which now characterises all Christian denominations, and which is a great feature of all East London places of worship is indeed amply provided for at St. Mary's, and that, too, in a way which shows how Evangelicalism is able without compromise to take full share of the latitude which is now so commonly assigned to congregational utterance in church.

Sunday evening at St. Mary's is a still larger and more notable demonstration of church-going, and the scene is one of the most encouraging sights which East London can show. The church is filled with at least a thousand persons of the working and poorer classes of Whitechapel. The beautiful and impressive service is an experience not to be forgotten. The sermon, too, is redolent of the place and the people. In the evening the vicar applies himself to the actual circumstances and difficulties of the congregation he knows so well. Here it may be mentioned that the population of the parish is twenty thousand, and that every family of this large number, Jew and Gentile alike, is regularly visited by the rector and his assistant clergy. Mr. Sanders can accordingly put his hand at once on the ills amidst which his people live.

Mr. Sanders' picture of the underpaid industries of Whitechapel and the results in bodies and souls of the unfortunate workers contributes important data for a view of the problem from the Christian standpoint, and seldom have the responsibilities of society in this matter been stated with greater power and wiser sympathy.

> ' Oh, if our brother's love cry out at us,
> How shall we meet Thee who hast loved us all,
>   Thee whom we never loved, not loving him !
>   The unloving cannot chant with seraphim,
> Bear harp of gold, or palm victorious,
> Or face the Vision Beatifical.'

Sunday afternoon is also an occasion for meetings in church for closer dealings with the industrial classes. The Pleasant Sunday Afternoon movement, in its higher aspects, has been commenced with much success. A gospel address from one of the clergy, the services of an excellent orchestra, reinforced by the fine organ of the church, with popular hymns and sacred solos, attract a class who seldom otherwise see the interior of a beautiful church, or hear sacred music in which they can join, or get into close personal touch with the clergy. The *imprimatur* which the rector of such a parish has freely given to this new development of the Sunday afternoon service is naturally felt in East London to be a great encouragement. Certainly in no part of London could crowded streets give a better mandate for these social gatherings as conducted at St. Mary's.

The Sunday schools of the parish are in the front rank of the church's work. They are situate in five different quarters of Whitechapel, Jewish and Gentile alike, and are attended by more than one thousand children.

The large number of Jews and foreigners in Whitechapel is naturally felt as a claim upon the parish church. Special services for Jews are held on the principal Jewish festivals. The prayers and lessons are read in Hebrew and German, and sermons are preached in English and Yiddish (Judæo-German). Between four and five hundred persons are present on these occasions.[1]

The picturesque and admirably placed open-air pulpit is a valuable means of reaching the many passengers by this great East London highway. The large open space of the parish churchyard, where it is placed, is in free communication with the public footway, so that the wayfarer is easily attracted within earshot. Addresses are given every Sunday evening in the summer months at 8.30. On Saturdays at 5 P.M. there is an address to Jews. Most of the addresses are given by laymen. The pulpit was erected in memory of the late Dean Champneys, one of the most famous of Whitechapel rectors.[2]

The Universities Settlement, known as Toynbee Hall, may naturally be expected to figure in a description of a Whitechapel Sunday. In what form, it might be asked, does it contribute to the religious activity of the day? Toynbee Hall is situate in almost the centre of the Jewish quarter, and is entered from Commercial Street, the great thoroughfare which unites Spital-fields with Whitechapel High Street. By its side stands St. Jude's Church, of which one of the leaders of the Universities

[1] The large and almost incredible number of important evangelical, educational, industrial, and mission agencies which are at work on week-days in the parish do not come within the scope of this paper. They are detailed in the rector's annual report.

[2] During the present year Mr. Sanders has left Whitechapel for Dalston, and has been succeeded by the Rev. John Draper, from St. Paul's, Bethnal Green.

OPEN-AIR PULPIT
ST MARY'S WHITECHAPEL

Settlement project, Canon Barnett, was for many years the vicar. Opposite to St. Jude's is one of the most notable chapels of a former generation, the Baptist Chapel of which the late Charles Stovell was for many years the famous minister, and to

TOYNBEE HALL
THE COURTYARD

CLOCK TOWER

which he drew by the solemnity and force of his preaching a large and influential congregation.

The visitor will be disappointed if he expects to find Toynbee Hall a directly religious agency established for evangelistic purposes, and undertaking or assisting in church work on

Sundays. It should at once be said that the word 'mission' does not occur in its programme, although the intense glow of the inner personal life of Edward Denison, the leader of the movement, is still felt in the settlement. It was in 1867 that Denison, an Oxford student who had been profoundly impressed with the gulf existing between the rich and the poor in London, took lodgings near the London Hospital, and tried to share his life with the poor of the district. His example was contagious, and by the year 1874 it had become the custom for a few Oxford graduates to spend part of their vacation in the neighbourhood of St. Jude's, Whitechapel, and to join in some of the work of the parish. Among them was Arnold Toynbee. The intensity which Denison and Toynbee threw into their teaching and example made a great impression on public opinion, and the settlement at Toynbee Hall took an organised and permanent form in the year 1884. From that date up to the present time its scope and aims have been ethical, social, and educational, and within the limitations thus adopted its character and achievements have become well known. Toynbee Hall is a lay settlement, and, in the words of its programme, its object is to 'provide education and the means of recreation and enjoyment for the people of the poorer districts of London.' Toynbee Hall 'has become a name under which a society holds together, formed of members of all classes, creeds, and opinions, with the aim of trying to press into East London the best gifts of the age.'[1]

What the Sunday visitor is looking for he will find more or less realised in another University Settlement which exists a little farther north, at Oxford House, Bethnal Green. At Oxford House, as we shall see, in addition to the object sought at Toynbee, there is a distinctive church mission working on Sundays in aid of the parish churches around, as well as providing, out of church hours, definite religious teaching and holding religious services. The delivery of a gospel message to the vicious, the sin-worn, and the heart-broken, and of rescue from sin and judgment, as prior to all other objects in life, is recognised here and at other settlements in East London. But

Annual Report, 1893.

at Toynbee Hall such agencies are not now contemplated in the plan of the institution.

Looking at the Jewish character of the district, it is not improbable that Sunday science and literature classes may be much more extensively developed. Already the Museum attached to the Whitechapel Free Library is open on Sunday afternoons, as a concession to the enormous proportions of Jewish residents, and is attended by as many as sixteen hundred persons every Sunday. Sunday classes have already been opened at Toynbee Hall in literature, physiology, botany, and other sciences.[1]

The most eventful of the changing conditions of religious life in Whitechapel as affecting the future is the decline of the old sources of voluntaryism among the population. This is seen chiefly in the serious diminution in the number of the Nonconformist chapels of various denominations. It is also making itself felt in the greater difficulty of raising funds for the parish churches. The causes are not far to seek. The great diminution in the number of large employers of labour whose aid could formerly be reckoned upon, and especially the disappearance, owing to fiscal changes, of the great sugar refiners, may be cited as one, although not the most potent, of these causes. Spacious warehouses now stand empty and roofless, or are transformed for other purposes by companies and corporations who have no personal ties in the district. The further explanation is to be found in the decrease in the English population of the district, and, above all, in the almost total disappearance of the middle class, who do so much for churches and chapels elsewhere. So far has this decline proceeded that even the endowed churches can only be held by clergymen who have private means of their own, or who can obtain help from friends in the more distant and the richer parts of London. Only by means of outside

---

[1] Here and elsewhere in this series of papers, aims and agencies are reported as entering into and colouring the life of the population, and as thus indicating some of the deeper changes which are proceeding in East London, and some of the newer conditions under which Christian work has now to be carried on. In this respect some account of them is indispensable to a working knowledge of the East End Sunday.

subsidies from a few wealthy and generous Christian donors is it found possible to maintain the truly noble and multifarious work which is carried on at Whitechapel parish church.   At present St. Mary's is maintained in its old and vigorous continuity by appeals of the rector to a circle of friends in other and richer parts of the metropolis.   Only by these means is the great annual deficiency of some thousands of pounds made good, and the very varied and onerous ministrations maintained at the needful strain.

The ever increasing Jewish population of Whitechapel, apart from the social morass of the inner Ghetto, is rapidly becoming Anglicised, and the process is being attended with serious results to the older indigenous English residents.   Indeed, the last-named are being steadily pushed out of their native quarters by the irresistible competition of the new-comers.   In the light of this portentous fact, the struggling and precarious condition of Christian organisations of all kinds, which need money for their support, will be still better understood.   From this rapidly multiplying Semitic population, to whom Whitechapel is an El Dorado, aided by the powerful and highly creditable efforts of the West End Jews not only to humanise but to Anglicise the Ghetto, some twenty thousand Jewish children are being daily equipped for the industrial market in East London.   In two or three years, all these children will have been launched into local industrial life, with an obvious result upon the balance of races and the competitive conditions of labour.   The humbler standard of living and expenditure common to the poor Jew, in a district over-populated, and the increased keenness in competition for work, tend inevitably to displace the Gentile population of Whitechapel and the adjoining parishes.   The process will continue probably at an accelerated rate, greatly to the religious and economic transformation of East London.   We shall meet with further illustrations of it in our future glimpses of Sunday in East London.

III

GEORGE YARD, WHITECHAPEL

GAIN, on a Sunday morning, we stand in the grand and spacious highway, market-place, and *piazza* in which Whitechapel most loves to congregate. Nearly opposite Whitechapel Church and its beautiful church-garden and open-air pulpit, we shall find the modest street-frontage of the George Yard Mission. The numerous hospitable invitations in the window assure us of our destination. Alongside of it is George Yard itself, entered by a roofed gateway. Within, we soon find ourselves in a district which is in strange contrast with the spacious, busy, and cosmopolitan High Street, with its rural-looking hay-market.

George Yard backs on to the great common lodging-house area of Whitechapel and Spitalfields. Wentworth Street, where the magnificent Gothic frontage of Toynbee Hall and its Balliol and Wadham Colleges stand in strange juxtaposition with the habitations of outcast humanity, may perhaps be deemed the headquarters of the George Yard district. Here is one of the hugest of these East London barracks of the homeless. In the lofty four-storeyed Wildermauth Buildings, some four hundred men sleep every night. Wentworth Street is still the haunt of the hereditary vagrant class, as it was fifty years since. Thrall Street, just beyond it, is marked in Mr. Charles Booth's Map of East End Poverty as the centre of a settlement of the vicious and semi-criminal classes of East London.

It is significant of the character of the district and the urgency of mission work that the Salvation Army was born in the year

1865 not far from George Yard, at Buck's Row, where, in a chapel now pulled down, Mr. Booth established the Christian Mission, out of which grew the world-wide organisation of which he is now the head.   To-day, as we shall see, the Salvation Army is still in possession, although in newer premises, in Wentworth Street.

We enter the George Yard Mission premises by Angel Court, and find ourselves amidst a large group of buildings, not visible from the street, and almost puzzling in their labyrinthine variety. The venerable Mr. Holland—' George Holland,' as he is familiarly yet respectfully known through the length and breadth of Whitechapel—kindly comes forward, white-haired and slightly bowed with the weight of his threescore years and ten, and offers to be our guide.   The multifarious buildings are soon explained.   The simple ragged school of 1856, we are told, was soon compelled to open out into a wider Christian mission.   Such were the overwhelming claims of Whitechapel in those early times.

Only a summary of the well-known and honoured work of the mission, as given to us on the spot from Mr. Holland's lips, need here be recorded.   The work among the children comes first. The day nursery for the 'buds,' the Sunday and week-day schools for children in the higher stage, the children's service on Sunday morning, and the Bible classes for those who have reached riper years, fill some of the various rooms and halls through which we pass.   The evangelistic service for adults on Sunday evening, at which we were present, is perhaps the most impressive sight of the day, bringing together many of the men and women in middle life, once scholars at George Yard, who owe their salvation to the mission.   Altogether in the busy season some eight or nine hundred are gathered here every Sunday.

But there are many other agencies not seen by the casual visitor.   The Sunday evening services at the lodging-houses around, the Shelter in which children are taken from the evils of the common lodging-house, and where they are housed, fed, and clothed until they can be got into employment; the Bible and industrial classes for rough boys, the social meetings for the factory girls, the admirably-equipped Gordon Hall, Shaftesbury Hall, and Kinnaird Institute, all tell of fruitful branches of work hardly contemplated in the humble beginnings of the simple one-room ragged school. But we will ask Mr. Holland to speak for himself.

COLLEGE BUILDINGS
WENTWORTH STREET

'The lads and girls of Whitechapel take a foremost place in your affections, Mr. Holland; but what do you consider your chief work?'

'The children, unquestionably,' replied Mr. Holland, 'are our first charge. For them the mission was established. It was for the children that my greatest friend and adviser, the late Lord Shaftesbury, was always pleading. George Yard was one of his favourite missions, and his last words were a solemn charge to me never to desert the children.

'That monument,' continued Mr. Holland, pointing to his Shaftesbury Hall Memorial in Angel Yard, 'is an ever-present pledge to the best friend the mission ever had, and to the children who are its chief charge.'

'Where do the children chiefly come from?'

'Many of them,' said Mr. Holland, 'are from the common lodging-houses around. But you would not know it. We do not believe in dirt and rags, and in a short time we get them suitably cleaned and clothed.'

Here Mr. Holland stopped a little fellow who was passing, and who in appearance and speech showed himself an excellent object lesson of the George Yard methods.

'Our day school, composed of these children,' continued Mr. Holland, 'takes a good position and gets a Government grant; but only from the George Yard circle of Christian workers should I get such teachers, who, though certificated and able to command double the salary they get here, choose to stay with me. Who else would actually wash and make wholesome the new-comers from the slums—the little street arabs for whom George Yard exists?'

'Your work, Mr. Holland, will be a memorable page in the early history of London home missions. How and when did it begin?'

Mr. Holland replied: 'You will find the first printed notice of the George Yard Ragged School in Mayhew's *London Labour and the London Poor*, published nearly fifty years since. The writer saw me, in those early days, at the head of a drum-and-fife band in the streets of Whitechapel. Yes, out of our earliest ragged scholars we had formed a band of musicians, and were traversing the streets in the way since made so popular by the Salvation Army.

'I should say,' Mr. Holland continued, 'that George Yard was started as a mission for the whole of East London, until the vast scope of the work gradually dawned upon us.'

'Who were your helpers in those early days? I think some well-known public men were associated with you?'

'Yes; and many of them have gone to their rest! First and foremost I must name Lord Shaftesbury, who loved East London as few men have ever loved it. Hugh Allen, too, as vicar of St. Jude's, was always at my right hand—indeed, he led me to take

GEORGE YARD MISSION
AND RAGGED SCHOOL

up this work in preference to going into the ministry, for which I was preparing. Then there was the rector of Whitechapel, Mr. Champneys, the father of us all; and Samuel Thornton. Dr. Tyler, too, one of the best-known men in East London, was almost my earliest friend. Lord Harrowby and Mr. Samuel Morley were too among our benefactors.

'Of the godly and noble women,' continued Mr. Holland, 'who have greatly helped me, the names of Miss Marsh, Mrs. Chalmers, Mrs. Ranyard, Lady Kinnaird, Mrs. Gordon (daughter of Snowdon Henry), and many others, occur to me. Only two or three of these are still living, but happily the place of the departed ones is being nobly filled by the ladies of the present generation.'

After some further conversation, we gladly accepted Mr. Holland's suggestion that we should visit some of the common lodging-houses of the district.

'We hold short services in the common kitchen of these houses,' said our guide, 'every Sunday evening, of course paying all respect to the privacy of the inmates. The way in which we are received would be a lesson to those who think the lowest class in London are alien to the gospel, or hostile to its missionaries.'

One of these houses is in George Yard itself, and we started to visit it forthwith. The plan of the interior—in the small and large lodging-houses alike—is the same. Entering the common kitchen, a large hospitable fire greets the visitor; benches and narrow tables are ranged alongside the walls. A religious service, conducted by Mr. Holland's assistants, was proceeding at the far end of the room, whilst the precincts of the fire were left free for the cooking and eating, which, in the case of a few of the inmates, were proceeding quietly at the same time. Women and a few children were amongst the lodgers, the house being licensed for married couples.

The simple, hearty, and brotherly service was over in twenty minutes.

'We don't forget,' said Mr. Holland, speaking of the audience, 'that this is their home, and we are only here on sufferance; it would be a grave mistake to take up their room and time too long.'

'And they do not resent your visits?' we asked.

'On the contrary,' said Mr. Holland, 'if we neglected them a single night, they would very soon be sending down to us and wanting to know the reason why. In fact,' Mr. Holland con-

tinued, ' I never find nowadays any difficulty in getting a hearing for the gospel among the very mixed classes who fill the lodging-houses, who are, it must be admitted, largely of the lowest type of humanity. It is true we have had to live down a great deal of opposition. Years ago life in George Yard was almost intolerable, so rampant and woeful was the vice which hemmed us in and tried to scare us out of the district. But that time has passed. The mission has conquered, so far as getting the confidence of the people is concerned.'

Wildermauth Buildings, to which we next direct our steps, is the great caravanserai of the district. This is the gigantic, newly-built common lodging-house, with dormitories for four hundred men, of which mention has already been made. Like its smaller neighbours, it is the hostel of the very poor, who can only afford the threepenny fee for the night's lodging. No questions are asked, and the homeless and characterless human débris of the great city here find a refuge unmolested and un-challenged. The lofty and capacious building is exceeding well constructed for its purpose, and marks a great advance on the common lodging-house accommodation of the East of London. At the request of the proprietor, Mr. Wildermauth, it was publicly opened by Mr. George Holland some few years since with a short religious service, and a few words of congratulation and affectionate exhortation, such as would only be accepted from one whose name is a household word in the lodging-houses of Whitechapel and Spitalfields.

It is eight o'clock on Sunday night when we enter the great common room which serves for kitchen and sitting-room. Here are assembled all the four hundred inmates, for the most part sitting solitary and listless. The outdoor resources for spending the day are now exhausted, and as the men sit here, bereft of all family ties, and mostly wrapped in their own isolation, the scene is a sad one. But here, as elsewhere, common lodging-house life is not neglected by the world without. As we wait, a company of the Christian Community arrives, to cheer the inmates with a musical service. The orchestra seem specially acceptable to the poor belated ones, and the gospel service which follows speaks to attentive ears of peace and blessedness through forgiveness and reconciliation. Here, as at the neighbouring lodging-house already described, any intermission of the Sunday night service would speedily lead to a message of inquiry at headquarters on the part of the disappointed inmates.

The influence of the George Yard Mission extends far beyond Whitechapel. As a stimulus and encouragement to workers in other fields, its value has been abundantly and gratefully acknowledged. All classes of society have sought to give their aid, and have felt and acknowledged a reciprocal benefit. Among Mr. Holland's cherished tokens of sympathy and goodwill is a gift of two of her favourite books from Queen Victoria, on a fly-leaf of which Her Majesty has been pleased to inscribe with her own hand a gracious and kindly message to the venerable superintendent of the mission. The Duchess of Teck has long been one of the mission's constant friends and benefactors, taking a direct part in the work. Many other influential helpers might be mentioned. The Homes near the Shirley Hills, in Surrey, consisting of three cottages for the reception of the very poor for a fortnight's rest, are the gift of Louisa Lady Ashburton. In the same beautiful country is the Mary Baring Nest for children, the Ashburton Rest for grown-up persons, the George Holland Dovecot for mothers and their babes, and the Prophet's Chamber for weary workers.

The George Yard Mission has indeed been happy in its founder and superintendent. Long before the times of University Settlements of laymen in East London, he had adopted the principle of living day by day among the poorest of his fellow-men, and sharing their untoward and in those days almost intolerable surroundings. After half a century spent wholly in Whitechapel, Mr. Holland carries with him secrets of East London life and character known perhaps to none else in all their solemnity and pathos. The story of the sadder and darker side of humanity may well be deeply written on his heart. Yet Mr. Holland's success is one of the noblest and most inspiring in the record of East London missions : his fellow-workers in neighbouring fields rejoice to know that no name amongst them is mentioned with greater love and homage. Workers so dissimilar as Canon Barnett, Mr. Archibald Brown, and Mr. J. G. Adderley alike delight in the counsels of his large experience and in gaining fresh inspiration from the deep springs of his inmost religious life. To attract the regard, if not indeed the reverence of his fellow-workers, and at the same time to be the tender and beloved shepherd of the poorest and most outcast children of Whitechapel, is indeed not to have lived in vain.

Grateful as George Holland expresses himself for the love of those whom he seeks to serve, he points us elsewhere for the sufficient strength by which he has been carried through so many generations of strenuous and unspeakably anxious work. In a few words of gracious farewell to his visitors, he points them to the favourite motto which adorns the walls of George Yard—

'These forty years the Lord thy God hath been with thee ; thou hast lacked nothing.'—Deut. ii. 7.

IV

KING EDWARD MISSION

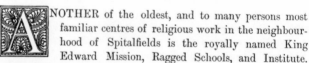NOTHER of the oldest, and to many persons most familiar centres of religious work in the neighbourhood of Spitalfields is the royally named King Edward Mission, Ragged Schools, and Institute. We are not sure that the term ragged school should not have first and foremost place, for a ragged school it was fifty years ago, when it originated, and ragged school still forms the centre and the core of its work. An average attendance of 1520 children of all ages throngs its classrooms on Sunday, including morning, afternoon, and evening school. The term 'children' is here very elastic, for it includes young persons up to twenty-five years of age.

'But how do you manage to keep these elder pupils?' we ask Mr. Montague, who has been connected with the mission from the first, and is now the honorary superintendent. 'How can you retain these young people of twenty and upwards?'

Mr. Montague has no cut-and-dried answer, but his reply makes it clear that one bond is found in the wholesome social work which goes on during the week. They have grown to like the place, to like their teacher, and probably to be influenced by what they have heard, and so on Sunday they find their way hither. There are no fewer than four hundred young people between the ages of sixteen and twenty-five connected with the institution, and most of them have been in the schools from infancy. Here, for instance, is a large class of factory girls, and here, in another room, a large class of working lads, all of whom we suppose to be earning their own living. They appear decently dressed, and no doubt take advantage of the savings bank of the institute. On a Sunday evening the whole building seems like a busy hive ; and the hum of voices, and the singing of hymns, and the instruction of the teachers, resound from floor to floor of the large structure. There are probably eleven hundred pupils of various ages gathered here.

But in addition to the classes, mission services are also held on

KING EDWARD RAGGED SCHOOL AND INSTITUTE.

Sunday morning and evening at King Edward Street, and in the afternoon at Albert Street. For there are two large buildings belonging to the mission, one in each of the streets named, but quite close together. Thus there are three services for adults on the Sunday, and also a men's Bible class—attended by men from thirty to fifty years of age, and conducted by the missionary of the institute. There are, too, large mothers' meetings early in the week. The Sunday services are conducted by students from Dr. Grattan Guinness's College at Harley Street, Bow, and by missionaries from Mr. Spurgeon's Evangelistic Association.

'And why,' we ask Mr. Montague again, 'why do these good people prefer to come here to attending a regular church or chapel?' Again the superintendent has no one answer that might be supposed to reply to the whole question. 'They seem,' he says, 'to be more at home at these mission services, and unfortunately they do not appear to understand the ritual, or the forms of the services at the churches or chapels. Then there are their clothes; oh, I can assure you the people do not like the idea of being put into a back seat—oh no! We opened a reading-room during the week, and that seemed to break the ice, and drew them to the institution.

'Then, further, we have been here now a long time, and, I suppose, have acquired some influence over the people. In addition to the services we have a prayer-meeting here for adults, from a quarter-past six till seven. Our largest attendance is in the morning, when we get, I suppose, about two hundred and fifty persons at the service.'

And where, it may be asked, is this Institute and Ragged School situated? He would have to be fairly well acquainted with the East End who would find it. Back behind main thoroughfares, some little distance from Spitalfields Church and bordering on to Bethnal Green, there in a labyrinth of streets you shall find it. A few of the old weavers' windows may still be seen here and there in the houses around, and Mr. Montague will tell you that he remembers the time when fine dahlias were grown in gardens hereabout. But gardens and dahlias have long since gone, as well as the 'field' in which Mr. Montague was wont to wander as a boy. This part of London seems now as full of bricks and mortar as the rest. But this very mission used to be housed in a cow-shed! 'Not many cow-sheds now in East London, we expect,' we remark to Mr. Montague, and the good superintendent agrees with us. Yet, strange to say, there appear to be more goats for sale in the curious Sunday morning street-market held in Club Row and its neighbourhood (which is not very far from King Edward Street) than in many a country town.

And yet another strange thing. As we are threading our way through the labyrinth of streets to these fine buildings, Hebrew placards look down upon us from windows and doors, Hebrew names are set forth on shop-fronts, Hebrew faces throng the streets. We feel inclined once more to ask—Is this really London, or some strange foreign city?

And everyone seems out of doors. Children, Christian and Jew, play in the thoroughfares, men and women stand beside their houses. There seems no disturbance, and no noise, but no one appears to think of going to church. The bells are calling for public worship, but no one here seems to think of church, and the children rush and skip and play, and the men and women loaf about and talk. And everything seems outwardly quiet and orderly and even respectable.

'A great change has come over East London,' we remark to Mr. Montague presently. 'Great indeed,' he answers; 'I can remember the time when there was fighting and gambling in the streets that now seem so free from disturbance.' But if the inquirer were to prolong his visit till later on in the evening, when the public-houses have been open sufficiently long to do some of their mischievous work, we doubt if he would find such quietude as now prevails. Close the gin-palace, and as a rule you gain outward order and quiet; open it, and in many places you may expect the disturbances of which you hear. But with the gin-palace open or shut, a wholesome change has indeed passed over East London. Later in the evening, in the darkening thoroughfares, you meet a large and empty brake which has taken a number of people for sixpence each out of the crowded streets a few miles into the suburbs or farther on into the country. In the summer cheap rides of this kind become a marked feature of the East End Sunday life.

And now, how did the present extensive King Edward Mission arise and grow? It was in November 1845 that the late Rev. Dr. Tyler, a Congregational minister, rented a little room in Ely Place, King Edward Street, as a ragged school. Mr. Montague, the present esteemed superintendent, was in that old little room as a boy. Then Dr. Tyler and Mr. H. R. Williams—who is now so well known in the North of London—took an old stable or cow-shed in Spring Gardens close by; and this palatial new departure was inaugurated by Lord Shaftesbury—then Lord Ashley—in 1846. It was intended to be a ragged school, and was such in sober reality in days when Board schools were unknown. Though provided by Congregationalists, it was unsectarian from the beginning, and has remained so ever since. Both Churchmen and Nonconformists are among the vice-presidents, and the late Lord Shaftesbury was president for nearly forty years.

The next step was to purchase a plot of ground in Albert Street, close by, on which the present block of buildings was erected and opened in 1851. Then, in 1853, the stable and a block of nine cottages, which were flanked by Ely Place on one side and Spring Gardens on the other, were purchased and pulled down, and a large mission building with classrooms erected on the site. So it happens that close together stand the two commodious structures for the one mission, and both appear fully used. In 1890 the splendid gymnasium was added to the Albert Street building; it is believed to be excelled by none in London, and is used on Sundays as a school. These large buildings, filled on Sundays with their large attendances, and the centre all the week of so many operations—from the lending of whitewash brushes and pails and the giving of materials wherewith people may cleanse their ceilings and walls, to the holding of numerous industrial classes for teaching needlework, carpentry, and other things—these large buildings and their wide and varied operations form an extraordinary development indeed of the little school in the little room fifty years ago.

And Mr. Montague has seen it all. That is, he has been connected with the work all the time. He was elected a teacher in 1854, and ten years later a superintendent, a post which he still holds. The present magnificent lending library work may be said to be the outcome of his personal efforts. During the cholera epidemic of 1866 he visited much in the homes of the people, and was greatly struck with the absence of reading matter in their dwellings. He applied to Dr. Manning, who was then one of the secretaries of the Religious Tract Society, and a grant of books was made to the mission to form the nucleus of a library. That Free Circulating Library has now so grown that upwards of 78,000 books or publications were lent or given away last year. In addition there is a free circulating library for boys and girls. Indeed, the energies of six librarians are now required to cope with the work, apart from the ten tract distributors, who are also connected with the mission.

Altogether over a hundred voluntary workers are engaged in the operations of the institute, for not only is it a busy hive on the Sunday, but all the week likewise something is carried on. Food is distributed in the bitter winter, excursions to the country are planned in the bright summer. A trained nurse is employed in attending the sick poor, and upwards of forty thousand visits were paid last year by the nurse, the Bible woman, missionary and district visitor. These are but a few of the agencies of the mission, and no doubt they have an important bearing on the Sunday work, for it is linked with it. Speaking of the work, 'We can point,' said Mr. Montague, 'to men now in important public positions, deacons of churches and so forth, who were brought up in our schools'; and no doubt the King Edward Street schools, with their average attendance of 1520 every Sunday, can present a record which will compare with that of any similar institution.

V

SPITALFIELDS

ISTORICAL Spitalfields, with its pleasant and inspiring memories of the Huguenot immigrants and
their traditional industries, still survives in the
London of to-day, though hardly pressed for life
under its changed conditions. The visible memorials of the
French weavers, and of not a few English worthies, are still to
be found there, even if in disguise. Newer London is rising here
as elsewhere, on time-honoured sites, with irresistible energy, and
well-nigh submerging the London of less than fifty years ago.
But the fine old houses of the more prosperous merchant weavers'
period still remain, savouring more of Bloomsbury than of East
London, so rich are they in oak-panelled rooms and broad stair-
cases with Grinling Gibbons' balustrades. In large gardens, once
owned by well-to-do weavers, are still shown the mulberry trees
of the Huguenot days, when the silkworms were fed on the
home-grown leaves.

The weavers' dwelling-houses have changed hands, and the
industry has well-nigh fled; but the long latticed windows of
the top storey, right under the eaves, so as to gather for the looms
the amplest daylight, still remain to tell their tale. Nor is the
district poor in biographical interest. At No. 3 Wood Street
lived for many years Dr. Isaac Watts, the famous hymn-writer,
when the house was the school premises of the Protestant Dis-
senting Charity, of which he was a director. A flagstone long
marked the site of the mulberry tree under whose branches he is
said to have composed many of his well-known hymns. The

CHURCH ARMY

FOR YOUTHS

LABOUR HOME

BRANCH No 14

HOUSE FORMERLY
OCCUPIED BY
Dr ISAAC WATTS

55

doctor's study is still shown to visitors. In the once prosperous Church Street, where nearly every occupant used to keep his carriage, may still be found the once famous *Neuve Église*, the largest of the Huguenot churches in Spitalfields. Here, in later times, when the church had changed hands, John Wesley preached more than once to nearly two thousand hearers. In Hanbury Street, close at hand, is another of the Huguenot sanctuaries, the famous La Patente. Here may still be seen the historic and

SPITAL SQUARE

admirably carved and painted coat-of-arms granted by Royal licence, authorising the use of the building for the Huguenots' services. It is now a mission hall for Christ Church, having been purchased for that purpose by Bishop Billing, the former rector.

The fine parish church stands like a great lighthouse in these darker days of the decaying fortunes of Spitalfields, when the scenes over which it towers lie in a deeper darkness than it has perhaps ever known. Yet here also old Spitalfields is curiously linked to the present. The early morning bell, which used to ring out from the lofty tower to call the weavers' apprentices from their beds, still rings daily at a quarter to six, and the curfew is still rung at eight at night.

Spitalfields is not an easy place for the stranger to find, and he may have to ask his way more than once. It lies obliquely off the greater highways of Eastern London, between Whitechapel and Shoreditch; and it backs on to Bethnal Green. Entering it about church-time from the northern or Shoreditch approach, by the new and imposing thoroughfare known as Commercial Street, we meet a few groups of the church and chapel going classes. Most of them are making their way to the Rev. William Cuff's great Shoreditch Tabernacle; others are making for the fine parish church, St. Leonard's, of which the Rev. Septimus Buss is the well-known rector, and others for St. Stephen's, Spitalfields. Passing the beautiful new building near Quaker Street, known as the Bedford Institute (the famous East London Home Mission House of the Society of Friends), we speedily arrive at Central Spitalfields. Here the broad thoroughfare gets still broader, and exactly fronting Spitalfields Market stands the noble parish church, flanked and backed by the spacious and beautifully foliaged church-garden. The same goal may be reached by a West End or South London visitor by entering from the Whitechapel side of Spitalfields.

The days of the church-going classes in Spitalfields would almost seem to have ceased. As we look on this great central thoroughfare, Commercial Street, there is scarcely a sign of them. The more ominous days of a vast encampment of nomads and aliens have set in. The twelve Huguenot chapels of the last century have all been closed, or taken over for other purposes. The Nonconformist chapels have all gradually died out. So great have been the social changes and the lack of the means, of voluntary support. Christ Church parish church has now a population of 22,000 souls. As we stand at the magnificent church portico on Sunday morning, the bells above us are ringing out their invitation for service, but the sound is like an echo of the past. A few of the more abject of the population come to sun themselves on the spacious esplanade, or sit in the beautiful church-garden, where there are shine and shade, trees and flowers, for the evil and the good alike.

Even as a holiday thoroughfare, Commercial Street has none

CHRIST CHURCH
SPITALFIELDS

of the aspect of its livelier and more prosperous neighbour, High Street, Whitechapel, where there is always a populous promenade of well-dressed Jews and Gentiles. In Spitalfields, people, for the most part, spend a shiftless day in their own

narrower streets and byways, or while away their time in the
great Sunday all-day market in Wentworth Street. On a fine
summer Sunday, the place is deserted of the younger, the better-
clad and better-fed, who mostly make their way through Bethnal
Green to the nearest open space and recreation ground, Victoria
Park. The scarcely middle-aged as well as the elderly seem to
hang about their homes and street-doors the livelong summer
day, as if hopelessly settled on the lees of melancholy lives.

Let us turn again to the parish church. It is a grand building, well worthy of a great metropolitan parish. It has seating
accommodation for eleven hundred persons. Built in the year
1729, at a cost of £60,000, it is an imposing structure of almost
palladian grandeur ; but, alas ! the congregation seldom numbers
more than two or three hundred. Nor does the newly-erected
neighbour church of St. Stephen, with equal seating accommodation and more modern and attractive exterior, obtain a
larger congregation. And yet the swarming population around
often amounts to two thousand and more per acre, whereas the
figures shown on maps of the district not ten years old give a
proportion of four hundred per acre.

The Sunday aspects of Christ Church might easily mislead the
stranger to the parish as to the real strength and effectiveness of
the church in the district. Some extracts from an interview
with Mr. Scott, who succeeded Dr. Billing, the Bishop of Bedford,
will throw considerable light on the situation.

' It may be presumed, Mr. Scott, that your Sunday congregations by no means represent the nature and results of your work
in the parish ? '

' They certainly do not. In the first place, it has now become
quite impossible to build up a congregation here. It is not
simply that the people are in the depths of indigence ; it is
because they are a population of nomads, here to-day and gone
to-morrow. Last year, over eighty per cent. of the poor who
came under the Poor Law of Spitalfields Union were non-
resident—that is, had no homes of their own. It is like building
upon a morass ; everything you put in disappears, and your
foundation is never laid.'

'And inasmuch as it is a non-church going population, your work is chiefly a campaign, outside the church, in all parts of the parish?'

'Yes. When I came here, Bishop Billing, my predecessor, said to me, "Yours will not be sanctuary work!" I soon found out what he meant. We have to decentralise our church, so to speak. As the people do not come to church, we have to go after them and plant out all kinds of church agencies among them.

'Yes,' Mr. Scott continued, 'our mission work out of doors and in common lodging-houses, the personal visitation of every street by the five clergy and seven mission women, and especially the rescue of fallen women, more than keeps our hands full. At least three hundred lost women are recovered year by year by our excellent lady missionaries. Trying as the work is, isolated as we are from humane and Christian society and sympathy, in this terrrible flat of poverty and semi-barbarism, we are content so long as we see some fruits of our labours.'

'But all these agencies cost money, and you tell me your offertories in this great church do not exceed thirty shillings a Sunday. Yet you spend—and therefore raise—some four thousand pounds a year!'

'Yes, the work demands that amount at least, if we clergy are to justify our presence here. I am not the only rector in East London who has to collect some two thousand pounds or more outside his parish every year from his own personal circle, in order to make both ends meet.'

'Do you think things are getting worse?'

'I am afraid so. The separation between East and West is unquestionably more marked year by year. And we have no resident employers of labour on a large scale to help us. The well-to-do are conspicuous by their absence; the rich are not with us to contribute to our offertories; the educated are not here to teach in our schools; it is impossible to find ladies to visit in the district; and while the rector sees his responsibilities daily growing, the poverty around him is steadily deepening.

'Close by us,' continued the rector, 'is the notorious Brick

Lane, "a land of beer and blood," as the late Mr. Montague Williams called it; and not very far from my own door, Jack the Ripper perpetrated some of the worst of his unspeakable crimes. Sometimes I have to stop free fights under my own windows.'

'Yet you find inspiration in your work?'

'Oh yes. We accept our mission, and live in it and for it. And there is much to hearten and encourage us. Many of the poor are very grateful, and we do see some result of our labours. Moreover, we are planted here to hold the fort, and succour the country, and hold up the beacon-light until better times—in any case, to spend and be spent for our fellow-men.'

After an allusion to the successful Pleasant Sunday Afternoons at the mission hall, Mr. Scott went on to mention the greatest of all the difficulties he has to reckon with—the number of foreign Jews settled in Spitalfields. These amount to at least twelve thousand, or one-half of the entire population of the parish. Several missionaries are daily employed in visiting the Jewish quarter for evangelistic purposes.

On Sundays and other days when the greater Jewish festivals are observed, large congregations of Jews are assembled in the parish church, to a service conducted in their vernacular—the Judæo-German tongue.

'See the Spitalfields Ghetto for yourself,' said Mr. Scott, 'and you will have an idea of the limitations to our work, as well as the claim of the people.'

Leaving Christ Church behind us, we cross the road for the Jewish quarter. In less than two minutes the almost unspeakable scene is before us. We seem to be in a world of dissolving views. We suddenly find ourselves in a foreign land. The street we enter might be a street in Warsaw or Cracow. We have taken leave of everything English, and entered an alien world. Wentworth Street—that is its name—is even a greater Sunday-market than the better-known thoroughfare of which it is a branch—Middlesex Street ('Petticoat Lane'). It is the market of the thickly-herded, poorer immigrant Jews—the Ashkenazi Jews from Poland, Russia, Germany, and Holland.

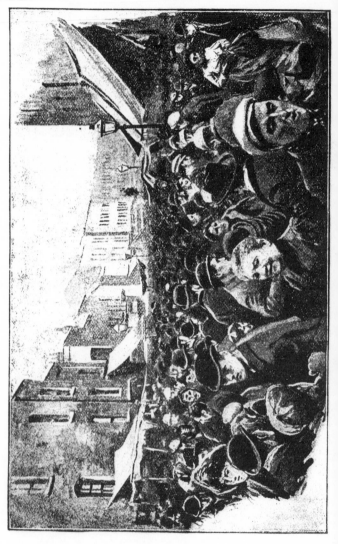

It is the East London counterpart of the poorest and meanest of the Continental Ghettos, minus the gaberdine and the more picturesque architecture. Whilst other Sunday markets close not later than noon, the Spitalfields Ghetto-market goes on the livelong day with unabated vociferation and energy, and lasts long after the evening church-bells have ceased. In the heart of London, it is yet like a foreign town, with its own liberties of trade, its own segregated peoples, religions, customs, and industries. Here is seen that great phenomenon of the deeper poverty, the poor living upon the poor.[1]

Strange as it may seem, there are no scenes of disorder, and nothing approaching to ruffianism. The people are peaceable and law-abiding, and give no trouble to the police who watch the thoroughfare ; they seem wholly absorbed in the sordid struggle to meet to-day's wants.

Such is a Sunday glimpse of the population of twelve thousand who now divide Spitalfields with the English casual. The fact that the invading race gradually settle down and hold their own, superseding the lower class of Londoners, is full of significance. The difficulties of the parish clergyman, who sees his nominally Christian parishioners excelled in civilisation, in morals, and in the social and civic virtues by a people of an alien religion, are proportionately increased.

But the Ghetto is full of surprises. Close by the social swamp of Wentworth Street a far different aspect of Judaism presents itself. We stand in front of a magnificent pile of buildings, right in the heart of the Jewish quarter. This is nothing less than the Bell Street Free Jewish Schools. Here is gathered, week by week, probably the largest Sunday school in the United Kingdom. There are at least three thousand children within its walls. As we stand outside, we listen to the hum of multitudinous voices. The children are receiving instruction in the religious classes which are so great a feature of the Jewish Sunday in East London. The Christian visitor who gains admission gazes on

[1] Herr Sokolow, the editor of the Hebrew daily newspaper, *Hazefirah*, of Warsaw, recently visited the ' Polish market ' in Wentworth Street, and remarked that there was nothing so dirty to be seen in Warsaw.

the scene with puzzled admiration and almost incredulity. The splendid classrooms, the fine central hall, the complete equipment of the building for the thousands of little ones and their teachers, and the signs of almost unlimited resources and the most careful provision, are everywhere apparent. If he has just seen Judaism in its lowest forms, he sees it here in its strength. The schools are, in fact, the largest of the schools for elementary education in the whole kingdom. They were built at a cost of £90,000. The principal benefactor is Lord Rothschild, who takes a practical and leading part in their management, and visits them week by week.

The poor Jewish adult immigrants are chiefly a burden upon the community, but no pains are spared to train the children to the London level of educational attainment. The powerful hands of the able and extremely earnest leaders of London Judaism are hardly anywhere so apparent as in the work at Bell Street.

Let us now turn to another and very different type of Sunday life in this strangely-mixed quarter of our world metropolis, in which men and institutions of divers races and religions are living together and working out their several ideals side by side. We are now to make acquaintance with the Quakers of Spitalfields, the Society of Friends, who, on ground of their own choice, and with methods peculiarly their own, are doing excellent work in this part of London.

The Bedford Institute, a very attractive-looking building, is the headquarters of the Society of Friends' Home Mission to East London. Established some thirty years since, and just rebuilt on a larger scale, 'The Bedford,' as it is familiarly called, embodies the beneficent ideals of its founder, the late Peter Bedford, silk merchant, of Spitalfields. It also marks an eventful departure in the spiritual polity of the Society of Friends. The idea of mission work, which it so conspicuously realises, was by no means a received and orthodox tenet of the society when the Bedford Institute was founded. Nevertheless, in a very short time the enterprise rallied round it many sympathetic and influential colleagues. To-day not only is the Bedford Institute one of the most valuable centres of Christian work in Spitalfields, but it has sent out vigorous ramifications into nearly all quarters of East London.

The visitor will find the Bedford Institute situate near the Shoreditch end of Commercial Street, Spitalfields. It is flanked

THE BEDFORD INSTITUTE

by Quaker Street and Wheler Street. In Wheler Street was the historic meeting-house where George Fox, William Penn, George Whitehead, and other leaders of early Quakerism were wont to assemble, during the years from 1656 to 1700. In 1755 the site passed into other hands. But the Bedford Institute, built as

near as possible to the spot, worthily sustains the cherished
traditions of its seventeenth-century predecessor. The lofty,
picturesque, red-brick building, with its gables and tall roof, is
constructed and equipped with the solidity and liberality and
far-sightedness which distinguish all the admirable buildings
erected by the trustees.

The Sunday begins with a well-planned hospitality to the
destitute of the district—a free and substantial breakfast to the
poor, whose poverty is nowhere seen in a more aggravated form
than in Spitalfields.

Provision is made for two hundred, who are supplied with
tickets of admission by those who well know the district, and the
poorest of its lodging-houses, and the hiding-places of those who
are ready to perish. The large lower room in which they are
received and comfortably seated is built for the purpose, and is
itself a lesson in cleanly living as well as of hospitality. After
grace is sung, the hungry ones are amply fed, and the bearing
away of a portion to the breakfastless ones at home is acquiesced
in by the kindly givers of the feast, but not before a prayer is
offered, a hymn sung, and a few short and brotherly addresses
delivered for the guidance, cheer, and help of the departing
guests. A temperance society, a labour agency, and rescue homes
are all in requisition at these useful gatherings, and the testimonies of their value week by week are more than enough to
encourage those who conduct them.

The Sunday schools follow the breakfast. These are for boys,
girls, and infants. A notable feature of the teaching of the
elder scholars is the use of copybooks, so that the Scripture
lesson is at the same time a writing lesson.[1] The copies chosen
are Scripture mottoes or texts bearing upon personal religion and
conduct. The classes meet again in the afternoon. In the
schools connected with the institute more than two thousand
children attend. In the evening the children are gathered to
listen to short addresses and to join in worship, the service being
made as simple and engaging as possible.

[1] See 'Sunday in Birmingham,' *Sunday at Home* for March, 1894 pp.
293–346.

By far the most important outgrowth of the Bedford Institute is to be found in Hart's Lane, Bethnal Green, a little distance from headquarters. Here there are no less than seven hundred children in attendance at the beautiful and admirably equipped building known as the Friends' Hall. This large number of little ones is superintended by no less than one hundred and twenty teachers. There is also an adult school after the Birmingham model, meeting at 8 A.M. Evangelistic meetings are held morning and evening, and there is an outdoor meeting at the end of the evening service.

Those who are unaccustomed to associate evangelic fervour and missionary zeal with Quaker methods would be agreeably surprised if present at one of these gatherings. Here is a picture of the First Day School at Hart's Lane. The speaker is one of the young women who shares in the teaching of the seven hundred children :—

'It is very touching in our senior classes to see the young people there on prayer-meeting Sundays, and hear them pleading earnestly in their own simple way that the Lord would help them to live holy lives in their homes, to stop the angry word and to curb the hasty temper. Some of us know what it is to be the only one in the family who is trying to serve the Lord Jesus Christ. We know how difficult it is, and feel our need then of living very near to Him. We do desire that our hearts may be filled to overflowing with His love, that it may flow out to the dear ones whom we try to get on the Lord's side. Sometimes we see in our classes the tear quietly fall while lessons are going on. We inquire the cause. Sometimes we are taken into full confidence, and find it is a little trouble at home. You see how we feel the need of living near to the Lord ourselves, and our earnest desire is to be able to point these dear ones to Him who said, "Come unto Me, all ye that labour and are heavy laden, and I will give you rest."'

The Sunday-morning school for men, meeting as early as eight o'clock, has already been mentioned. The Bedford trustees are anxious that it should be as great a success in London as it is in the Midlands and the North. In London, the late hours of the Saturday night tend to destroy the value of the Sunday morning for any religious or serious purpose, and are among the greatest evils which the clergy and church workers generally have to complain of. Accordingly, the Bedford Institute trustees provide inducements for early rising on Sunday. The handsome and costly structures assigned and built for the 8 A.M. Sunday school are situate in Bunhill Row, and are known as the Bedford Memorial Buildings. There is an average weekly attendance of some three hundred men, out of a membership of four hundred on the books. The movement is regarded by the promoters as being almost in its infancy in London, but it is viewed by other religious workers in the locality with a watchful sympathy, which will not improbably be a prelude to imitation, to the further advantage of Sunday morning observance in Spitalfields.

Such are some of the aspects of the Quaker Mission in Spital-fields. The memories and traditions of the Huguenot weavers and their ancestors could scarcely find a worthier embodiment than the Bedford Institute. But the Bedford Institute is more than a memorial ; it is a Christian mission, and, in the frequent words of one of its leaders, 'mission work has now become an essential part of vital Quakerism.'

VI

SHOREDITCH AND BETHNAL GREEN WEST

IN no quarter of 'Darkest London' is there a more evil and sorrowful record of the lives and squalors of a miserably housed and overcrowded population than in Western Bethnal Green and Shoreditch. In no part of the vast metropolis have the powers of evil more boldly challenged the labours of the city missionary and his fellow-evangelists and the civic authorities; and yet no district of London has a more inspiring history of mission work prolonged and carried on through successive generations. The central stronghold of this hard-fought battlefield is easily described. It is close upon High Street, Shoreditch, one of the chief of London's thoroughfares. Eastward it stretches towards the notorious Brick Lane, Spitalfields, and on the south a Sunday visit would show it to be in close touch with 'Bird Fair,' the greatest of ornithological Sunday markets.

This is the unhappy district known to-day as the 'Boundary Street' area. Here, until lately, was one of the last surviving London rookeries of the older type. Foremost for many years past among the 'slums' of the metropolis, it has at length exhausted the patience of the civic authorities, and its thirteen acres of slum tenements are now razed to the ground, as utterly unfit for human habitation. A new model village is now taking its place.

A Sunday visit to the locality will easily discover some of the brighter as well as the darker spots in the chequered picture. Only two or three hundred yards away from the condemned area Lady Burdett Coutts's great and beneficent enterprises cluster around Columbia Market, and stretch out a helping hand to the poorest. Here, too, entrenched for more than sixty eventful years in the worst part of the area, is the Duthoit Ragged School Mission, the beneficent foundation of one of the Huguenot merchant weavers. Here also we shall come upon Christian enterprises of later date, such as the magnificent Mildmay Mission Hospital and Poor Man's Home ; and last, but not least, Miss Macpherson's admirable and far-reaching mission, the Home of Industry. Here again is a church memorable under more than one vicar for its mission work in the worst days through which the district has passed ; we mean St. Philip's, Bethnal Green. Quite as near to the most dangerous and indigent byways of the district, the Rev. Osborne Jay carries on his labours for the very poorest of the population through his church and its associated lodging - house agencies.

Nearer to Shoreditch Church we shall find well - equipped mission stations, which remind us again of great lighthouses and beacons and rescue agencies for a people who mostly live a hard and perilous life in threatening and storm-tossed waters. We shall not fail to be struck with the great Shoreditch Tabernacle, one of the gladdest sights we shall see, which stands close by the stately and graceful parish church. Nearer at hand, too, the newly-founded Shoreditch Mission Church of the Wesleyans will also come under our notice.

Evil as are the annals of this part of Bethnal Green, there is yet, as we shall see, no part of reawakening London which presents more remarkable features of Christian activity.

It is Sunday evening. Spitalfields, which we visited in the morning, has merged into Shoreditch. We are no longer in a by-thoroughfare, but in one of the chief of London's highways and holiday promenades. Nowhere do the swarming, holiday-keeping population of North - East London congregate more thickly on Sunday evenings than at the confluence of metropolitan roads which has Shoreditch Church for its landmark. The spot is one of the traffic-centres of London, and is akin to the meeting of the ways at the Angel at Islington, or the Elephant and Castle in Southwark. Tramways, railways, and omnibuses feed it from all quarters. The chief tributaries are the Hackney Road (now sunk to the social level of average East London, and quite a new and needy claimant for mission work), the Kingsland Road, Haggerston, Old Street, Curtain Road, and populous Hoxton.

Shoreditch and the Hackney Road are crowded with holiday-makers, for we are at the great meeting-place of old and new London. Here decaying yet over-populous suburbs press on towards the thriving main avenues which end in Bishopsgate Street and Cornhill. In the by-streets and roads right and left of us, we get glimpses of great human warrens, the huge 'models,' as are popularly called the lofty piles of industrial dwellings now so prevalent in East London. These are the barrack-like structures which transform a single street into a great village, so far as population is concerned, and immensely increase the density of the human settlement per acre.

Our goal is the Shoreditch Tabernacle in the Hackney Road. Here we shall find one of the most conspicuous mission churches of East London, under the charge of its founder and minister, the Rev. William Cuff. The Tabernacle is only a few yards from Shoreditch Church, and a steady stream is setting in towards its hospitable doors. But the non-churchgoing aspects of the crowded holiday-making thoroughfares for the moment eclipse all other thoughts. Public-houses abound, and as the evening wears on, their beacon-lights and open doors are all the more conspicuous amid the general Sunday closing of the shops ; they plainly tell of the more popular social centres on the Sunday evening.

It is a startling fact, suggestive of the scanty home provision, that the rural deanery of Shoreditch, which covers but little more than a square mile, contains more than three hundred licensed public-houses.

Still more startling is the decline in church-going habits. The population of the ecclesiastical district is 62,000. But at a census of the attendances at the Established churches on a recent

Sunday evening only 997 persons were present. There were 5433 seats unoccupied.

Through the open doors of Mr. Cuff's great Tabernacle, throngs of the better class of well-dressed working-people are passing and taking their seats. There are no rented seats in the spacious

SHOREDITCH TABERNACLE

building; all comers alike are welcomed, and before service begins a congregation of some three thousand has assembled. The preacher occupies a pulpit platform, with a large and competent choir on a gallery behind him. The singing is supported (not led) by the organ. From the choir gallery behind the preacher the congregation presents an impressive scene. The majority are young people, in the first flower of their age, for Mr. Cuff is a favourite with the young, as the overflowing Sunday schools adjoining attest. Yet the opening extemporaneous prayer, with its deeply-sympathetic petitions for the aged and the sorrowing, gives full assurance of a large-hearted pastorate for old and young alike. The sermon has for its high aim the salvation, sanctification, and full equipment of man for the service of God and his fellow-men. In method as well as in aim, the preacher's great natural gifts show the happy influence of his exemplar, the late Mr. Spurgeon. He dislikes oratory, in the rhetorical sense of the word, and contents himself entirely with simple, unaffected speaking to the heart. He has the frankness and ease which Mr. Spurgeon so happily introduced into the modern pulpit, but which so few can command in dealing with large audiences.

Mr. Cuff, it should be said, has no belief in the extra attractions which are now provided to induce the people to come to church. ' We have not even any Pleasant Sunday Afternoons at the Tabernacle,' he says, 'and I think it can be proved that this movement does not attract working-men to the regular service of church and chapel.' (Mr. Cuff makes some exceptions, but this is his judgment of the average meeting.) He adds : 'I do not object to a bright service, indeed, I pride myself on the fact that our Tabernacle services are among the brightest in London. My people not seldom laugh and cry by turns. But preachers must be thorough and true to themselves. In their brightest moments the solemnity of their mission weighs upon their hearts.'

The Shoreditch Tabernacle's outside agencies bear witness alike to the fruitfulness of the pastor's preaching and the generous services of the many lay helpers who are inspired by his teaching and his example. The Sunday school numbers no less than thirteen hundred children. The beautiful octagonal school-building, with conical roof, clerestory, gallery, central hall, and separate bays cut off for classes, is one of the most notable and best equipped edifices for its purpose in the kingdom.

Eight mission halls have been established, and the services are carried on by working-men. At the head of them is the historical chapel in Gibraltar Walk, once the 'Nonconformist cathedral' of East London. Here is shown the Morley family pew, where the late John and Samuel Morley, who afterwards became London merchant princes, were wont to sit on Sunday with their father and mother in the early years of the century, when the chapel had more rural surroundings. It has been taken over by Mr. Cuff for the branch work of the Tabernacle, and is a fully-manned mission, in which the poorer mothers and children are specially cared for, not to speak of its appreciation and use by working-men.

Every Sunday, at least three hundred workers in the mission field give themselves to the outside agencies of the Tabernacle, visiting, teaching, or preaching. Such is some of the work in which the pastor of Shoreditch Tabernacle has now been building up for a period of twenty-two years.

It would nevertheless be misleading if in the presence of so fertile an oasis of East London we lost sight of the social wastes which lie around in appalling need and with miserable insufficiency of spiritual supplies. None are more painfully aware of the spiritual destitution of the district within the half-mile radius of the Shoreditch Tabernacle than the pastor himself, notwithstanding his twenty-two years of persistent labours. 'The work of my Tabernacle and all its branches,' says Mr. Cuff, 'is but as a drop in this great ocean around. The burden oppresses me more and more. The whole district is getting poorer. My congregation once consisted of well-to-do people, but now these have moved away. We are full with an almost exclusively working-class attendance. I love them, and mean to stand by them. But, alas, that our fellow-Christians at the West know so little of the burdens which lie so heavily upon us in the East!'

Until the year 1893 the Shoreditch Tabernacle stood alone as a great mission citadel in the district. A new and vigorous colleague has now entered the field. The new-comer is the Wesleyan Shoreditch Mission. A connexional chapel had already existed in the Hackney Road for many years. In the year 1890 the Wesleyan Home Mission Committee took charge of the chapel, and sent the Rev. Samuel Wilkes to work it. Mr. Wilkes found the place well-nigh deserted, but after two years of toil he succeeded in getting a settled Sunday evening congregation of some five hundred persons. During Mr. Wilkes's term of nearly three years, the mission character of the work was largely developed, and the buildings were further adapted to this end. The Rev. S. Chadwick took up the work so successfully founded, having left his ministry in Leeds to devote a year to the purpose, and during his stay his remarkable pulpit gifts proved to be a great attraction. In 1894 he was succeeded by the present minister, the Rev. J. H. Maddock. The Sunday services are attended upon a scale which much impresses the visitor.

The mission chapel is situate in the Hackney Road, a few hundred yards distant from the Shoreditch Tabernacle. The district on either side of the main thoroughfare is extremely poor. The chapel is described by Mr. Chadwick as 'in the midst of a dense and very mixed population, who agree upon few things, save their indifference to religion. But if they are indifferent to religion, the grim spectre of starvation, ever present at their doors, takes good care they shall not be indifferent to the many and varied fluctuations of capital and labour. With many of the best, life resolves itself into one long, fierce struggle for bread, and with many of the worst into utter abandonment of all effort, except to get the oblivion or exhilaration of drink. It is against this colossal indifference to religion that the missioner must fight with unshakeable faith and untiring persistence, and buoyant cheerfulness that simply will not go under.'

In the morning the visitor will find a larger congregation here than any in the neighbourhood, except that of the Shoreditch Tabernacle. Yet only by degrees was this result achieved. The late hours of rising on the Sunday morning have to be reckoned with here as elsewhere, so persistent is the habit of the average London working classes of not breakfasting until eleven on Sundays, and dining between two and three. In the afternoon, which is getting to be more and more an occasion throughout London for adult meetings, especially in the winter months, there is a gathering of some four hundred to an adult Bible class. Regular attendance is encouraged by prizes at the end of the term.

On Sunday evenings the mission chapel is packed some time before the hour of service with a congregation of nearly a thousand persons. The singing is hearty and general. Here and at the kindred mission centres in East London, great importance is attached to the choice of hymns. The older and more memorable compositions in the history of missionary Methodism still hold their place in Wesleyan mission services as well as on ordinary occasions. One of the most solemn and affecting, as sung by the large congregation, is that which sometimes closes a service which has been more successful than usual in reclaiming wanderers or bringing new disciples to the fold. Such is the favourite hymn—

> ' All things are possible to him
>   That can in Jesu's name believe.
> Lord, I no more Thy truth blaspheme,
>   Thy truth I lovingly receive ;
> I can, I do believe in Thee,
>   All things are possible to me ! '

Hymns of the more recent mission character are also occasionally used ; and many are the happy confidences which the mission preacher sometimes receives after the singing. It needs but a little experience of mission work in Shoreditch to discover the freshness and power of hymns so familiar as to appear to be hackneyed in ordinary religious circles, but which often have a startling effect on crowds who have never known the spells of sacred song and the graciousness of the gospel message.

The work of the Sunday is maintained during the week with social and devotional agencies, visitations, and meetings. The present superintendent is the Rev. J. H. Maddock, of Plymouth, a town which has given to Methodism Dr. Pope and

Dr. Dallinger, and which is rich in Methodist associations of every kind.

The Shoreditch Union of parishes, with its 120,000 inhabitants, is noted for its great churches and the activity of the clergy in charge of them. In nearly all of them the seats are free, and the industry and assiduity of the church workers, both lay and clerical, in visiting the poor and educating their children, might be supposed to be effectual in bringing in the working classes.

The churches are conspicuous and commanding edifices. They are of almost mediæval massiveness of structure, and with the school buildings, clergy - house, and mission room, often cover a very large space of ground. The cost of site, building, and internal equipments is very considerable, amounting in three or four instances to at least £20,000.

St. Michael's, near Curtain Road, on the Finsbury side of Shoreditch, occupies, with its ample group of associated buildings, the whole side of the street. The church seats 800. St. Chad's, Nichol Square, has seats for 900, and St. Columba, Kingsland Road, for 800. St. Augustine's, Haggerston, has 940 free seats, and is the headquarters of various guilds, companies, brotherhoods, wards, and sisterhoods. The number of Sunday-school children on the books is 900. St. Mary's seats 1200 (free) ; St. Paul's, 1250 (1000 free).

In seven of the churches, the services are of the highly ceremonial and sacramental character which is believed by the several vicars to be not only 'Catholic,' but suitable and attractive to the poor. Incense, vestments, the eastward position, and the other observances which constitute the 'six points,' are adopted. In the other two churches, altar lights and the eastward position are adopted. On the other hand, two churches retain the simpler and more evangelical forms of worship : St. Mark's, Old Street, with 650 free seats, and All Saints, Haggerston, with 1100 seats, 600 of which are free.

At the morning service the adult congregation in several of the largest churches mentioned ranges from fifty to one hundred. The school children, who may number some two hundred, constitute the greater part of the assembly. Nor is the attendance at the Evangelical churches much more satisfactory. At the parish church of St. Leonard, which provides 1000 free seats, the morning congregation seldom exceeds 200. The evening attendance, which in all working-class districts is more numerous, falls far short of an average of 100 persons at each church. At the twenty-one churches of the district, many of them of very large size, the evening attendance on a given Sunday in the year 1894 did not exceed fifty persons at each church.[1]

The general neglect of church and chapel, and indeed indifference to religion in any form, is as freely acknowledged in Nonconformist circles as among Churchmen. It must, however, be remembered that these figures are no measure of the religious influence that is exercised, or of the work that is actually done. We are speaking of Sunday aspects, but the mission work is an everyday service. The ministrations of these various churches take many forms, and the gospel of Christ is declared and illustrated in many a life of which the world hears nothing.

Our visit to Spitalfields and Whitechapel has given us a view of the great Ghetto-market of East London on Sundays, in which the Jewish settlers in their thousands are the buyers and sellers. But a similar scene is equalled every Sunday morning of the year in a purely English quarter not far off.

This great English Sunday-morning market is in Brick Lane, Spitalfields, behind Bishopsgate Street Station. Here, close by the Bedford Institute, is the chosen spot where Spitalfields, Shoreditch, and Bethnal Green meet together to make the busiest and the poorest of these Sunday morning open-air exchanges. The market is entered northwards from Virginia Row, close by Lady Burdett Coutts's magnificent but unfortunate group of market buildings at Columbia Road.

The upper part of Brick Lane is solely occupied as a market for women, and here from eleven to one o'clock and later every Sunday morning they come in thousands to the stalls which choke the thoroughfare and the open shops which share the trade. The

[1] The authority for these figures is the Rev. T. Hodgson, Chaplain of Shoreditch Workhouse, in a recent contribution to the *Rock* newspaper.

BIRD FAIR.

roadway and the footways are as thronged as they are on the Saturday, whilst the crowds are even more eager for business. Boots and shoes and many other wares are spread out on the bare ground. The commodities are almost confined to the first necessaries of life : meat, bread, shell-fish, and vegetables. Dainties and superfluities are nowhere seen, and a rigid parsimony seems written on every face. The fair-like, holiday aspects of the Saturday-night market are entirely missing, and even the opening of a large wooden case of dolls excites no attention. The women are without head-covering, but are by no means of the very poorest of the population. There is no disorder, and no merriment, and apparently very little light-heartedness ; all are absorbed in buying and none in sight-seeing. It is comparatively a poor-women's market, but although the activity and crowding and eagerness equal if they do not exceed those of the Ghetto farther East, the poverty is by no means so great, and the standard of subsistence is evidently higher. Alas, that the extremely high rents which the poor are compelled to pay for even a single room in this congested district, and the impossibility of storing food under such conditions for to-morrow's consumption, should be the reasons given in so many cases for the existence of the great Sunday market of Bethnal Green !

Such are the Sunday - morning occupations of the great majority of the adult population in this neighbourhood. Suddenly a total change takes place in the character of the gradually-increasing throng. By the time we have reached Sclater Street, which runs across Brick Lane, not a woman is to be seen in the thoroughfare ; the crowd is composed entirely of men and lads, packed densely in the impassable street. The commodities, too, have changed, for we are now in the great bird-market of East London. The pigeon-fanciers of Bethnal Green and Spitalfields are in possession, and the street is blocked for hours, even the police finding it difficult to pass. Here again there is no approach to disorder. The public-houses are closed, and, as a policeman on duty is heard to remark, 'No beer, no trouble !' The seriousness with which business is pursued, and the eager interest taken by the vast throng in the proceedings, tells of the extraordinary place which pigeon-breeding still holds as the recreation and pastime of thousands of the poor, if not indeed as the chief object of their lives.

Here, then, are the missing thousands for whom the empty churches round so amply yet so unsuccessfully provide free sittings. Through the heart of this populous district, where Sunday morning brings nothing of its Christian benignities, the sordid human current surges with increasing volume as the years go on. It would indeed argue ill for the visitor if he were not moved more to grief and commiseration for these his fellow-creatures than to anger and hostility. The weekly spectacle is no new thing to the city missionary, the Scripture reader, and the district visitor. Happily, it is not the only side of human nature in Bethnal Green. We may well turn to some of the brighter and more ameliorative Christian agencies with which it is confronted, and which open up a more hopeful prospect.

At the corner of Club Row and Bethnal Green Road, exactly opposite the great open-air Sunday market already noticed, rises the lofty pile of new and spacious buildings now devoted to Miss Macpherson's Home of Industry. The pleasant sounds of the street mission service, with piano-organ and voices lifted in sacred song, have greeted us from the two mission bands which issue forth from the Home every Sunday morning. The splendid building in which the Home of Industry is now settled, after twenty-five years of service elsewhere, tells its story to all who pass by, with its gallery of pictorial placards and its large-text appeals for the higher life of virtue and godliness. It is now the headquarters of Miss Macpherson's manifold work. It is at once an industrial home, a mission centre, and a happily-placed rescue and recruiting station for the homeless waifs and strays who abound in the district. From Western Bethnal Green and Spitalfields come many of the lost and homeless lads who are taken into training at the Hackney Home, and eventually attain to honest and Christian lives and successful vocations in Canada, where Miss Macpherson has already planted out some six thousand East London destitute lads to flourish in a more hopeful soil.

At the Bethnal Green Home on Sundays the gracious work takes many forms peculiar to the day. Indeed, a Sunday spent at the Home of Industry and in accompanying the workers on their various missions will probably give a greater insight into the present-day condition of 'Darker London' than any other method which could be mentioned. The hours of the long day abound in evangelising agencies in a field of work where whole

HOME OF INDUSTRY
BETHNAL GREEN ROAD

armies of the non-church going populace assemble on Sundays on their accustomed camping-ground. From the early morning prayer-meeting in the Home, on through the morning crusade in Bird Fair, the afternoon Sunday-school classes, the night's mission services in the large lodging-houses of Bethnal Green, and the final gospel services to the masses in the large hall of the Home, the gracious task of bearing the gospel into the darkest scenes which London can show is carried on by Miss

Macpherson's band of workers, assisted by volunteers from all parts of London.

One who has spent a Sunday at the Home of Industry gives the following notes on the morning's expedition to the Sunday fairs and markets of Bethnal Green :—

'After breakfast is over, united prayer goes up for God's blessing on the labours of the day, and then we prepare to start. A small harmonium is wheeled along, and a little group of workers, each carrying bundles of tracts and illustrated papers. Another harmonium is left ready to be started soon after on another route. As we pass along, our hearts are saddened by the groups of unwashed women who stand about bonnetless, ragged, and aimless. After passing down one or two streets, we reach a wide railway-bridge in Brick Lane, under the cover of which preaching is carried on. It is a strange place of worship, we think, as we look around : it stands on the verge of what is called Brick Lane Market, where hundreds of women are just at this time doing their shopping.

'Soon a motley crowd is gathered : men with pipes in their mouths ; bonnetless women holding cabbages and other purchases in their arms just bought at the market; little children who have no Sunday clothes. After seeing the service fairly started here, we left to take tracts to the people in another market beyond. Alas, what a strange scene presented itself ! The shops all displaying their goods, the butchers shouting forth their invitations to buy, the whole of the narrow road lined with costermongers of all descriptions—all calling out the merits of their wares. Tracts were distributed and were well received, and conversation entered into. Invitations were given to all around to go and hear the preaching and singing beneath the archway.

'We left to pass through the streets where Bird Fair is held every Sunday morning. The Fair had hardly commenced, and men were pouring in from all points : we are told they come from miles around, bringing up choice specimens of birds, rabbits, fowls, and pigeons. At the end of the Fair we came into Bethnal Green Road, and here we found another railway bridge whose deep archway forms the second preaching station occupied by the workers connected with the Home of Industry and one or two members of the East London Evangelisation Society.

'We found the service had commenced, and we were thankful indeed to see how patiently the men stood, hardly any moving away through the whole service ; a strange variety of faces, some in respectable clothes with sunburnt faces, looking as if they might have walked many miles up from the outskirts of our great city ; others wore the dilapidated appearance so well known to those who work in the London lodging-houses.

'It was impossible to help looking round on this spot, which we mentally christened "Miss Macpherson's Cathedral," without feelings of the deepest interest for this dear worker, who has laboured here for many years with her faithful band of helpers.

'In the evening we prepared to go out on our mission to the lodging-houses : so again two bands and two harmoniums went forth. Imagine a long, low, narrow room turning round at the end in the form of the letter L. The ceiling and walls are both dark and dirty. On either side benches and tables are ranged, and on these benches the men lounge, some full length, smoking, others eating a meal which they have just prepared, some sleeping. Some are cooking at the fireplace, and ragged shirts are hung around the fire to dry. In winter, when the fires are roaring, the windows shut, the gas lighted, and from two to three hundred men are crowded on the benches, the atmosphere can be better imagined than described ! And yet the services go on, and the faithful messages of love and mercy are sounded forth in these dwellings, which contain to these men all that to them is meant by the sweet word Home. We felt thankful for the attention given by the majority of the men to the three gospel addresses and the singing of the hymns. At the close of the service a packet of illustrated papers were distributed, all receiving them most gratefully.

'The harmonium was then carried across to a Women's Lodging-House, and here only the lady-workers entered for the service. To *our* eyes it seemed even more sad to look at the group of dilapidated, hopeless women, than at the similar group of men opposite.

'A drunken woman staggered in while we were singing, and took her seat upon the benches with a drunkard's laugh; but when the address began she rose, and staggered out again. A little child with fair hair was playing about the room—alas! we thought what a home to rear a little one in. The place looked terribly comfortless, dirty tables covered with flies, and dirty benches round them, and ragged clothes hung here and there to dry; it seemed sad indeed that thousands of our sisters dwell in these abodes. We felt glad to hear that the Flower Mission from the Home of Industry carries a little brightness and sweetness even here. We felt indeed thankful to hear that an Association of Christian Workers from the various centres of mission work around has been formed for the regular, systematic visitation of these lodging-houses; so that everyone in the district (with the exception of two where entrance is denied) has the gospel proclaimed weekly in it.'

Such are some of the aspects of Sunday spent with the workers at the Home of Industry, Bethnal Green. The agencies have been left to speak for themselves, but the value of the Home as a training-ground for mission workers deserves special mention.

'From the Bible classes,' says Miss Macpherson, 'our most efficient young helpers for work in Bird Fair have been gathered; some of them are well able to tell out the gospel, sing, or play the harmonium. Others have become teachers in our Sunday schools. Several of them hold a weekly service in the open air, for preaching the gospel, all the year round. . . . While outwardly engaging in the service of the Lord in their spare hours, home duties are by no means forgotten. They care for their parents or their widowed mother in our busy East of London.'[1]

Miss Macpherson herself resides on the Bethnal Green premises in the intervals of her visits to Canada for planting out fresh colonies of lads who have been saved from London streets.

---

[1] Our quotations are made from the interesting booklet entitled *A Sunday at the Home of Industry* (29 Bethnal Green Road, E.).

Needless to say, her presence in a district of so many problems and urgent needs is welcomed by all Christian organisations as bringing strength to their forces. Seldom indeed is there seen so happy a combination as here of methods which have the

MILDMAY
MISSION HOSPITAL

promise of the life that now is as well as of that which is to come.

Close to High Street, Shoreditch, will be found two out-lying stations of the well-known Mildmay Mission of North

London. These are severally the Mildmay Lodging-House in Church Street, and the magnificent Mildmay Mission Hospital in Austin Street, at the rear of the parish church and the Shoreditch Tabernacle. Both institutions have, as may well be imagined, important bearings on the Sunday aspects as well as on the everyday religious and social welfare of the district. Their origin may be briefly told. In the year 1866, during the terrible visitation of cholera which then swept over London, and raged with unparelleled virulence in the East End, the overworked clergy knew not where to turn for help. In this emergency the late vicar of St. Philip's, Bethnal Green, Mr. Trivell, appealed to the Rev. William and Mrs. Pennefather of Mildmay, who gladly sent some deaconesses to his assistance. Many of the pioneers in this work still live to tell thrilling tales of the rescued ones who were brought out of darkness into light in those anxious and weary days, when the body's weakness became in a providential hour the soul's opportunity.

The lodgment thus made in the district was far too important to be surrendered, and measures were taken to gain a permanent foothold. A night school of street arabs was established under the superintendence of a deaconess, and persevered in under incredible difficulties and discouragement. A men's class was added. 'There were thirty scholars the first year,' writes our lady informant. 'Every winter the work became more and more interesting, and many of the men came out on the Lord's side. Some of them are now the heads of Christian households, having wives like-minded with themselves ; others entered the Army, and have witnessed a good confession in the noisy barrack-room ; one became secretary to a clergyman, and remained a long time in his service, and another is now a clergyman of the Church of England.'

How to employ these men permanently became a pressing question. It eventually led to the formation of a men's lodging-house and coffee-house. This provided a temporary shelter, from which they were gradually helped into situations. To-day the good work is continued in very commodious premises in Church Street, where the former handsomely built district police-station has been admirably adapted for its newer purpose, and made into a hospitable and comfortable lodging-house.

In such a district, where homes, alas! in the true sense of the word, are lamentably scarce, hardly a greater boon could be provided than such a kindly hostel as this, with its ample sanitary arrangements, its large kitchen and waiting-room, its coffee-bar, and above all its comfortable dormitories with sixty beds. The Sunday evening mission services here are among the brightest and heartiest of gatherings for the proclamation of the gospel. Indeed, throughout the week the same means are adopted every night for enlarging the humane work of the lodging-house, and widening its ministrations.

The amount of sickness around soon made it necessary to open a dispensary. But this was soon found to be inadequate ; nursing and proper food were required as well. A hospital must be added, and accordingly a disused warehouse was converted into a Medical Mission General Hospital. It was opened to admit patients on October 5, 1877. In the year 1882 the present magnificent Mildmay Mission Hospital with its three beautiful wards — 'Coventry,' 'Tankerville,' and 'Mathieson'—was opened, amid devout thanksgivings for the increased means of usefulness to the outcast around.

'Medical mission services are still held every Tuesday and Friday in a wing of the hospital set apart for the purpose. All the medicines used are compounded by the deaconesses on the premises. The deaconesses also treat all the minor surgical cases in the absence of the doctors, and carry forth to the sick out-patients tickets for beef-tea, milk, groceries, bandages, dressings for wounds, and materials for poultices. Nor are kettles and "Etnas" forgotten, for without them in many a desolate, fireless home, there would be little chance of hot water, either to wash the patients or prepare poultices.

'The gratitude of these poor people gives an access to their hearts that nothing else could give, and many lessons learned in sickness are turned to good account in health. But no accounts could exaggerate the misery, or exceed the suffering yet to be found in this one soul-harrowing district.'

'Your hospital work in the wards,' we ventured to remark, 'is of course a Sunday as well as a week-day work? It must be a doubly-hallowed time spent in so Christ-like a way of doing good on the Sabbath Day, especially in such a district?'

'It is a hallowed service which is laid upon us. Sunday is good for us and for our patients in the wards : it is the day when

> " The dawn of God's own Sabbath
> Breaks o'er the earth again,
> As some sweet summer morning
> After a. night of pain."

Many of our patients have said they never knew what a Sunday was until they had spent it in Mildmay Hospital.'

Much more could be told of the work which goes on in this noble building, so nobly served by the Mildmay deaconesses. Its inestimable value in a district where 'one-room families' abound, and where proper nursing, not to speak of the necessary nourishment, is an impossible luxury, will occur to every visitor. We take leave of the scene with feelings of the deepest admiration and thankfulness.

Again we turn our steps towards the 'condemned area,' the scene of desolation where to-day lie the ruins of some thirteen acres of 'rookery' of the most evil character which has stained the name of Bethnal Green. The almost quadrangular space on the accompanying map encloses the district in question, and shows the better-known landmarks which surround it. A few of the worst streets around still remain for a time, the miserable two-storeyed tenements, sodden and foul with the neglect of years and the occupancy of a nomad class, serving to show to the present generation a spectacle of the slum-London of the past. Here, especially in the three Nichol Streets, have been carried on for many years some of the most beneficent of Christian ministrations to a people terribly weighted by their almost inhuman homes and surroundings. It is only through such records as those of the London City Mission, with its sixty years of work, that the present generation can appreciate the devoted evangelical labours which have been spent in the

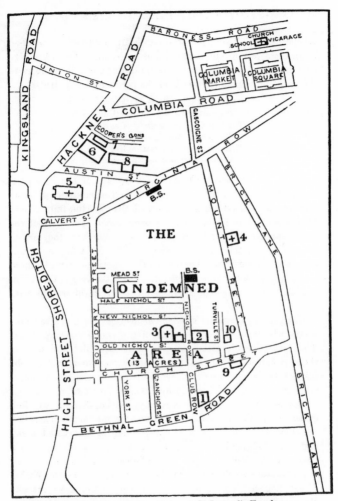

1. Miss Macpherson's Home of Industry.
2. Old Nichol Street Ragged School and Chapel.
3. The Rev. Osborne Jay's Church and Lodging-House.
4. St. Philip's Church.
5. St. Leonard's Church.
6. Shoreditch Tabernacle.
7. Lady Coutts's Cooper Institute.
8. Mildmay Mission Hospital.
9. Mildmay Lodging-House.
10. Mildmay Mission Rooms.

Nichol Street district.[1] As we look upon these half-wrecked houses, steeped in sin, sorrow, and suffering, we think of the city missionaries of London, and those unknown messengers of the gospel, to whom the words of the poet may be applied—

> ' Stairs to sin and famine known
>   Sing with the welcome of their feet ;
> The den they enter grows a shrine,
>   The grimy sash an oriel burns ;
> Their cup of water warms like wine,
>   Their speech is filled from heavenly urns.'

By no one are the trials and disadvantages of the very poor, as arising from their circumstances and surroundings, more readily and sympathetically discerned than by the faithful city missionary. The visitor to the district remarks : ' Few of the people in my district know from day to day how they are to live. The terrible struggle with poverty is in fact a prolific source of criminality. Apart from the question of drunkenness, my people are always in actual want, or on the verge of it. It is the daily experience of their lives : their children are born to it.'

Here, if anywhere in London, we feel the force of the words of the wise man, ' The destruction of the poor is their poverty.' The inevitable obligation to give judicious relief and help in these circumstances is realised by every mission agency in the district, but it is felt by the givers themselves that the problem is much too great to be solved by eleemosynary means.

Passing from Church Street into Nichol Street, we find ourselves in the presence of two notable missions. These are the Rev. Osborne Jay's new church and its associated men's club and lodging-house, and the far older, and indeed almost historical Old Nichol Street Ragged School and Chapel.

As far back as the year 1836, what are known as the Nichol Street Ragged Schools and Mission were founded by the late Mr. Jonathan Duthoit, of Highbury, a well-known Huguenot silk weaver. They subsequently became affiliated with Union

[1] See the *London City Mission Magazine*, September 1894 : ' A Review of Work in the Nichol Street District, Shoreditch.'

Chapel, Islington, of which Mr. Duthoit was a deacon from 1842 to his death in 1886.

The building, as may be seen to-day, was founded on a remarkable scale of liberality, so numerous, spacious, and commodious are the various halls, classrooms, and offices. The schools and mission halls have accommodation for 1400 children and 350 adults. The Sunday mission work begins with a free breakfast

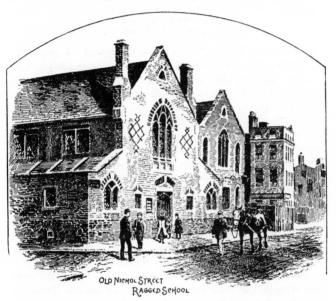

OLD NICHOL STREET
RAGGED SCHOOL

to the poorest of the children. The Sunday-school classes in the morning and afternoon are conducted by a band of workers from Union Chapel, and in the evening an evangelistic service is held. This is conducted by the city missionary of the district, or by one of the Islington leaders of the mission. An orchestral band and American organ assist in the hymns ; and the hearty singing of hundreds of voices is indeed welcome to ears chiefly accustomed to the far different sounds for which Old Nichol

Street has a bad eminence. Altogether, including the attendances throughout the day at all the services, some eight or
nine hundred children and adults use the schools and mission
hall every Sunday. To the late Mr. Duthoit and the congregation of Union Chapel belong the high honour of being the
pioneers of a social and Christian work in the parish which has
since been blessed with the admirable and more recent religious
agencies already mentioned.

Our notes on Sunday in Shoreditch would be incomplete
without a reference to the remarkable work associated
with the name of Mr. Osborne Jay. Mr. Jay's church
(Holy Trinity) is almost next door to the Old Nichol Street
Ragged School Mission just described. When Mr. Jay first
settled here, his parish was without a church to worship in.
Service had been carried on for nearly twenty years, first in a
stable, then in a hired room. A square piece of ground was
purchased and presented by a friend. The space so acquired
forms the basement of the church, and is used as a gymnasium
by the youths of the parish. Over this, on the ground floor, is
a large and lofty room, which serves the purpose of a club-
room in the evening, and a refuge and shelter for the destitute
by night. There are also two rooms which Mr. Jay himself
inhabited for a time, and where he can still find a night's
lodging when occasion requires. Over all, reached by a stair-
case from the street, is the church. Mr. Jay calculates that from
first to last he has collected for his church about £25,000, in sums
ranging from one penny upwards. Alongside the church, and
in connection with it, is a licensed lodging-house, where some
forty-eight beds and cubicles are nightly occupied by men
capable of paying fourpence or fivepence a night. Many of the
men attend church in the morning before leaving.

Perhaps the most interesting and affecting of the Sunday
gatherings at Holy Trinity is to be seen in the afternoon. At
three o'clock are assembled in the club-room beneath the church
the largest gathering of costermongers, casuals, and ' out-o'-works '
at any religious meeting of men in this part of London. Some
three or four hundred of this class, in which Bethnal Green

HOLY TRINITY CHURCH
AND LODGING HOUSE
SHOREDITCH

abounds—men who live the hardest and roughest of lives—come together with clean faces if sorry clothing, and spend an hour in the singing of favourite hymns to well-known tunes, accompanied on the harmonium by a lady mission worker. The rules of entrance to their afternoon 'club,' as the men like to call it, are not too stringent, so that those who keep their hats on, being unused to such gatherings, or even smoke a pipe, are not interfered with. Their behaviour throughout is admirable, like that of men who are gratefully enjoying in their own way the one really happy, social hour of the whole week, and recalling pleasures and associations to which they have long been strangers. As a rule they are homeless men, getting a night's quarters when they can in the lodging-houses around.

After the hymns they are invited to the four o'clock shortened service, with an address of a very simple and hearty character, in the church on the floor above. Many of them stay to this service or the overflow service, which is held in the club-room.

The mission is supported by Magdalen College, Oxford, which contributes £130 a year to its maintenance. Mr. Jay is unquestionably very popular with his parishioners, to whose interests he is thoroughly devoted, and in whose homes he is a familiar visitor.

A final glance may now be taken at the various mission agencies which we have thus passed in review. The richly varied work of the great Mildmay Mission, the far-reaching methods of Miss Macpherson's Home, the pioneer and present-day labours of the Huguenot Ragged School Mission, the beneficent parish work of St. Philip's, and the more novel but devoted and self-sacrificing efforts of the vicar of Holy Trinity, present a diversified picture of religious activity and service. It is, indeed, not too much to say that the district of Shoreditch, within the last few years, has been enriched with Christian missions to an extent hardly paralleled in other parts. With the rebuilding of the condemned area, and the rehousing of the population in worthier habitations, a better prospect begins to open. Meanwhile, in language already quoted, there are 'soul-harrowing' districts all around, and each new mission discovers a new field of unsuspected and useful work. It was after a Sunday spent among the scenes we have witnessed, that a visitor left on record these memorable words—

'Sorrow at the abounding misery and sin we had witnessed on every hand led us to a better understanding of that which stirred the Saviour's heart as He looked upon Jerusalem :

'"And when He was come near and beheld the city, He wept over it."'

VII

THE TOWER HAMLETS AND MILE END ROAD

HE great London highway which is known as the Mile End Road is no unworthy approach to an imperial city. In breadth, this grand main road of Eastern London surpasses the most stately of West End thoroughfares, not even excepting the historic road—the 'Appian Way,' as Leigh Hunt has named it—which reaches town through the Old Court suburb of Kensington. But here, of course, the parallel ceases. Mile End Road is comparatively unhistoric, and almost barren in monuments of the past. Yet in human interest, how largely it bulks in the view of the sympathetic visitor to East London!

The Tower Hamlets municipal area in which it is situate has at least a population of four hundred thousand inhabitants. Moreover, Mile End Road has become an important centre of the religious and social developments which mark the reawakening of East London. No quarter of the metropolis has a more interesting and striking record of evangelising mission work, and no part of the East London seed-field has been more consecrated and endeared by the untold labours of known and unknown husbandmen. In a Sunday notice of the district, we must necessarily leave out of view many established religious agencies which are helping to nourish the higher life of the people, for it would be beyond the scope of these pages to attempt a history or description of East London mission work in all its beneficent variety. An approximate picture of East London life as seen on Sunday is all that can be attempted.

To the stranger in East London, Mile End Road at any time

of the day or night is one of the great surprises of the metropolis. It is East London undoubtedly, but East London struggling, as it were, to come to the birth. Properly to understand its Sunday aspects and activities it should first be seen under its ordinary conditions. For this purpose any evening of the working-day which shows East London at leisure and out of doors will suffice.

The broad promenade—of all the broad highways of the metropolis second only to the Thames itself—is then the gathering ground, breathing space, market, and discussion forum of the liberated thousands of East Londoners—a great living picture-gallery of the street scenery of our Eastern Babylon. Saturday night, the night of the weekly fair and market combined, would be a still greater revelation.

More startling still is the spectacle when the great and rapidly multiplying Jewish population comes upon the scene, as on the eve of the Penitential Sabbath, or Great Day of Atonement. In the evening twilight, the whelming human tide begins to flow eastwards down the broad flat that leads towards the great Assembly Hall ; and it flows for hours. It is like the migration of a whole people. For the time, the populous Ghetto is deserted. In its Orientalism, the scene in the streets reminds the travelled spectator of the Eastern crowds of pilgrims at Jerusalem on the day of the Holy Fire. Every Jewish home at this solemn time is deserted of all but the very young children. Nearly all here now are poor, many of the women too poor to afford a head-covering. Many are aged and haggard, but all are absorbed in the overwhelming thought of *Yom Kippur*. They fill the huge Assembly Hall long before sunset. Of the vast concourse who seek admission, only ten thousand can find room, the largest congregation the Assembly Hall knows during the year ; other thousands have to be provided with temporary accommodation elsewhere.

On the two days of the Jewish New Year, Mile End Road is the scene of a festival and an assembly only second in solemnity to that of the Great Day of Atonement. On these days also the great Assembly Hall is hospitably lent in Christian sympathy with a people who have as yet no London cathedral or temple of their own sufficiently large for their needs. From sunrise till past the hour of noon the great building is thronged. At the close of the devotions we may see hundreds of Jews wending their way from the Hall to Tower Hill, and thence to the flowing waters of the Thames, where, as they hope, their wrong-doings of the past may be effaced as they stand in penitence by the river and utter the sacred words, 'Their sins Thou wilt cast into the depths of the sea.'

Such is the district in which we find ourselves launched on a Sunday morning. On our way, as we pass the Whitechapel Road, the first of the great Sunday mission agencies comes before us. This is the Pavilion Theatre, one of the most popular places of amusement in East London. On Sunday evening we shall find at least two thousand persons gathered here for an evangelistic service, conducted by the Theatre and Music Hall Sunday Service Committee. Expectation is quickened as we reach the great promenade which begins at the quaint historical Trinity Almshouses, a little east of the London Hospital. Here begins the strange succession of buildings which tells of the heterogeneous life of this part of East London. First comes into view the great Assembly Hall of the Tower Hamlets Mission,—'Charrington's Hall,' as it is familiarly but not disrespectfully called,—a building worthy of the West End in its stateliness and magnitude. Then follow Dr. Barnardo's Edinburgh Castle coffee palace, the once suburban and rural Mile End Congregational Chapel (now the great Sunday school of the Assembly Hall), and the Paragon Theatre of Varieties. After a brief interval comes Charrington's famous brewery, a great landmark for miles around.

Another gap succeeds, and then we are in front of the People's Palace, now the great 'Polytechnic for East London.' By its side is a church of world-wide celebrity; this is St. Benet's, Mile End, which has for its honoured vicar the founder of 'The Bible and the Prayer Union in All Lands,' with no less than 300,000 members.

Lastly, near the corner of Burdett Road, is the Rev. Archibald Brown's East London Tabernacle, one of the three great East End sanctuaries where congregations assemble in their thousands, and tell of the possibilities of churches and chapels even amidst present-day adversities in the eastern half of the metropolis.

So welcome and surprising is this great avenue through the heart of East London as to tempt us to forget the vast wilderness of houses which lie on either side. Yet there, out of sight, live the nine-tenths of the population who fill the mind of the city

THE PEOPLE'S PALACE

missionary and the church worker. To the left of us, over the houses, lies Bethnal Green, and to the south, Stepney, Commercial road, St. George's, and the docks.[1]

---

[1] The population of the Unions of parishes in the district in question, five years since, was officially given as follows: Bethnal Green, 130,000; Mile End Old Town, 120,000; Stepney, 63,000; St. George's in the East, 49,000.

The great Assembly Hall, the headquarters of the Tower Hamlets Mission and the central feature of the Mile End Road, is the first object of our visit. We must not, it seems, expect a large morning congregation even at this favourite Sunday resort. The great Saturday-night fair and market combined have closed the working week, and East London slumbers late on Sunday morning. It is nearly midday before the streets give any sign of the huge population which is housed around.

We enter the Hall with a steady stream of well-dresssed working-people. The scene within is extremely impressive. The building is not only beautiful and imposing; it is specially adapted for the worship of a vast assembly. It is capable of holding comfortably 4300 persons, and upon occasions it is made to seat fully five thousand. On Sunday evening it is well filled. The seats are entirely free, and hymn-books are provided. The service is quite simple and undenominational. It is conducted by a lay evangelist, who may be one of the permanent leaders of the mission, or Mr. Charrington himself.

The visitor will not fail to notice that the service and sermon, simple as they are, are deeply serious, and devoid of sensational methods. Indeed, from the first, Mr. Charrington and his colleagues have proclaimed and upheld this conception of the mission. 'The character of our mission,' wrote the late Ion Keith Falconer in its early days, 'is evangelistic, unsectarian, and sober. I say sober because of late years some seem to have despaired of reaching the masses except by using certain unseemly and sensational methods. Our work is an emphatic protest against this practice, and a standing disproval of its supposed necessity.'

But what, it may be asked, of the congregation itself, as representing the masses of East London? It may at once be replied that the visitor who has come to see a great gathering of the ill-clad and the destitute from the highways and hedges will be disappointed. The congregation is a well-to-do East End congregation greatly multiplied, except perhaps that there seems to be a larger proportion of well-dressed young people. The absence of the very poor and the destitute is not a pheno-

menon peculiar to this among other missions, and it will meet
us again in other mission halls, when it will be considered more
in detail.   Meanwhile, the great Assembly Hall Mission by no
means disowns responsibility for a class of young people so fully
represented in the congregation, seeing how large a number of
the same class are found on Sunday nights among the mere street
promenaders and holiday-makers of the Mile End Sunday
evening.   It is, moreover, fairly urged that the improving condition of many who attend the Assembly Hall is itself a result
of and testimony to the work done, and not a sign that the
mission misses its mark.

The scope of the Tower Hamlets Mission is by no means to
be judged by the Sunday congregations at the Assembly Hall.
There are outside agencies at work on Sundays and other days,
which greatly extend its range.   These agencies are in fact on a
scale of which the Sunday visitor can know but little.

The new Children's Hall, adjoining the great Assembly Hall,
is one of the impressive and inspiring sights of the East London
Sunday.   The total attendance at the various Assembly Hall
Sunday schools exceeds four thousand, and of these some eleven
hundred assemble every Sunday in the handsome building
formerly known as Mile End Chapel, which has been acquired
by Mr. Charrington chiefly for Sunday-school purposes, and
enlarged and adapted for its new uses.   The sight of a Sunday
school of more than one thousand children assembling in so
imposing a building is not easily forgotten.   It is not the least
of many testimonies to the hold which the Tower Hamlets
Mission has acquired in the family life of the district.

The relation of the work of the great Assembly Hall to the
churches and chapels around, and its effect upon their congregations, is an important subject.   The decay and disappearance
from East London of some twenty chapels of various denominations during the last twenty-five years, the absence of any
attempt to build new ones, and the low average of attendance
at other places of worship, nearly all of which are in a chronic
condition of struggle for self-preservation rather than for
aggressive work, have been contemporaneous with great social

changes. The notable decline of the East End middle class, which has already been mentioned, has very seriously affected the prosperity and stability of congregations. A conversation with Mr. Charrington's representative, Mr. Kerwin, who has now given twenty-five years to the work of the Tower Hamlets Mission, necessarily touched upon some aspects of this question. Some of the replies given to our inquiries may serve to remove some misunderstanding, and to place the work of the mission in a fuller light.

'It has been objected,' we remarked, 'that the success of the Assembly Hall is won largely at the expense of other and older congregations. Outsiders, it is said, have not been won to fill the building at all in proportion to the "spoliation" of church attendances elsewhere.

'It is also objected,' we continued, 'that the Assembly Hall is barely more than a Sunday preaching station, and that it does not follow up the services of the Sunday by pastoral work and organisation during the week. Is it true that the "miscellaneous crowd" who attend on Sunday are not shepherded from Sunday to Sunday, as is alleged, and that there is no social bond during the week tending to convert them into a settled congregation?'

'No,' was the reply; 'it is decidedly untrue, and there can be no excuse for so erroneous an impression, seeing that the facts are easily obtainable.'

'Do you publish any magazine or serial which shows what is going on, and the nature and scope of your work?'

'Certainly! Anyone can buy for a penny our *Illustrated Record of the Tower Hamlets Mission*; he will there see how comprehensive is the work of the one hundred and twenty agencies through which the mission ministers to the population of the Tower Hamlets.'

'What is the answer to the allegation that the Sunday work is not followed up by pastoral and parochial work during the week? Have you any kind of church organisation here?'

'Yes,' replied Mr. Kerwin. 'We have an organised church and a membership of two thousand. The Sacrament of the

Lord's Supper is administered twice a month, once in the morning and once in the evening.'

'And you attach great importance to church membership?'

'Yes; we are always putting it before our audiences. Our preachers constantly plead with those who have recently been brought to Christ to join themselves to some body of Christians. We say, "It is distinctly laid down in His Word that we not only join ourselves to the Lord but to His people. If you are not in fellowship with God's people, we urge you to join some church, ours or another. Do not go drifting about! You want a home. You cannot do without it for your temporal life, neither can you do without a home for your spiritual life."'

'And as to your alleged influence in attracting people from other congregations, and so weakening the churches and chapels around?'

'Our reply is first that we never accept members from other churches except in very special cases. Further, do the objectors, if there be such, know that our mission is sustained after twenty-two years by eminent Churchmen and Nonconformists alike—by supporters of both church and chapel? Moreover, is it really thought that with a ninety per cent. of non-church going population, an immense and unreaped harvest-field, we are to stay our hands and not put in the sickle?'

'I may take it, in fact, that the prejudice against your work is rapidly dying down?'

'You may! We are on the best of terms with all the neighbouring churches. The magnitude of the work is growing upon all of us. It is now felt that there is room for every variety of Christian enterprise, each church working according to its own special gifts.'

'And you look after the children of this immense district?'

'Our Sunday schools altogether number 4407 children and 105 teachers. The increase has been so great year by year that we have no longer room for them in the Assembly Hall, so Mr. Charrington has bought another large building close at hand. You have seen it? our new Children's Hall? Yes, the children of Mile End are a special charge of the mission. If anyone wants his heart melted by touching and beautiful sights and sounds, let him come to our Sunday morning or evening service, and hear a thousand children sing as with one voice one of their favourite hymns.'

Such is the latest development of the Sunday school in the Tower Hamlets. It may be remembered that not long since, Mr. Kirk, of the Ragged School Union, emphasised the importance of fresh efforts for the children of the East End. 'It is,' he said, 'a lamentable fact that religious organisations are not increasing their hold upon the rapidly multiplying child population.' This was his inference after thirty years of work in lifting poor ragged lads from the gutters of the streets. He longed to see the day when the places of worship should be open every night for the children.

'This,' says Mr. Charrington, 'is just what we purpose doing with our Children's Hall—opening it every night all the year round, just as our Great Hall is for adults.'

Some of the collateral Sunday agencies of the mission may now be mentioned. On Sunday afternoon, in the Young Men's Assembly Hall, which seats five hundred, there are meetings for men. There are open-air mission services in Victoria Park, the great forum of East London. At the great common lodging-houses mission services are held every Sunday night in the winter. The chief missioners are well-known residents in the district, and have the advantage of a knowledge of the circumstances of the people they address.

The Tower Hamlets Mission can now look back upon an eventful experience of more than twenty-two years. The beginning of the work, the earlier problems, and the able and gifted men who have devoted themselves to this great experiment in evangelisation are instructively described in one of the most interesting and inspiring of recent religious biographies.[1] The growth of

---

[1] *Memorials of the Hon. Ion Keith Falconer, M.A.*, by the Rev. Robert Sinker, B.D., Cambridge, 1888. In his ably-written pamphlet, 'A Plea for the Tower Hamlets Mission' (1882), Mr. Keith Falconer tells the interesting story of the commencement of the mission, and the way in which Mr. F. N. Charrington made the momentous choice of a career which has

the mission is primarily, under God's blessing, to be referred to the self-devoted efforts of Mr. Charrington. He found a most loyal and effectual helper in the brilliant student, scholar, and Cambridge Professor of Arabic, the Hon. Ion Keith Falconer, who died at the age of thirty-one, during his mission to the Mohammedans of Arabia, and whose memory is still cherished and honoured at Mile End.

It has been well said that every town has its training-ground, its school for workers. The 'wynds' of Edinburgh and Glasgow, the 'chares' of Newcastle, the 'crofts' of Sheffield: these are the kind of college which Christ's disciples cannot dispense with.[1] The remark finds a happy illustration in the recent history of East London in general, and of Mile End in particular.

'For more than thirty years,' writes the Rev. T. Richardson, the well-known vicar of St. Benet's, who has spent nearly this period in the district, 'the East End of London has been a scene of exceptional Christian activity. Probably it has done more than any other locality in London in the way of producing, training, and sending forth workers into all fields of the world. Thirty years ago its condition was deplorable, and its needs so great as to daunt and almost paralyse those who came to survey it for evangelistic purposes. Here was a world for workers to win, and certainly they have materially changed it in moral features and in social and religious life. To those who have had long and intimate knowledge of it, it is a transformed place. Mr. Charrington has gathered thousands of humble people together in Christian fellowship week after week for many eventful years. Dr. Grattan Guinness located his college here; indeed, he could not have done better.

'To go about in this neighbourhood is an admirable preparation for open-air preaching in India and China; to nurse the

been so eventful for mission work at Mile End. Mr. Sinker's *Memorials*, a book which is one of the classics of our home missions, incorporates these and other particulars, and is further valuable as showing the part taken in the work by the great Evangelical leaders of the day—Lord Shaftesbury, Mr. Spurgeon, Mr. Samuel Morley, and many others.

[1] J. P. G. in *The Christian*, June 28, 1894.

St Benet's Church
Mile End Road

A.R.Q.

sick is an apprenticeship for medical missionary work ; to gather the poor and needy and forgotten into societies is to acquire skill for handling any bodies of men and women anywhere. Two of the best qualified workers we ever saw sent into the Indian field had learnt their lessons about Mile End Road.'

The pulpit of St. Benet's, close to the People's Palace, is memorable as the place of the origin of the 'Bible and Prayer Union.' This world-embracing project began with the Rev. Thomas Richardson's repeated requests 'that every person attending that church should read the whole Word of God consecutively.' It has its ramifications in every part of the world and in every class of society. Started in the year 1875, it has now a membership of 320,000 persons in all parts of the world.

The Sunday visitor will not fail to notice that St. Benet's Church is one of the few handsome and cheerful-looking build-ings which, during the religious revival in East London, have risen to enliven the once sombre and unpicturesque Mile End Road. The adjuncts in no way bear out the general idea of an East End vicarage. The bright, modern church, built of warm-toned brick, stands next to the imposing buildings and spacious grounds of the People's Palace. The garden and cheerful vicar-age might have been transplanted from some retired rural parish fifty miles from the million-peopled metropolis. Its appearance does much to dispel from the West End mind distorted visions of the unbroken gloom of the far East.

Passing across the garden to the institute, one is initiated into the working of the Bible and Prayer Union. The register of membership is one of the most interesting of modern-world documents. The members are found in every class of society. Royalty, nobility, gentry, clergy, ministers of every denomina-tion ; undergraduates of universities, students in theological, missionary, and other colleges ; soldiers, sailors, policemen, post-men, merchants, tradesmen, artisans, inmates of workhouses and hospitals, are all represented. There are few more interesting records of an enthusiastic and world-wide propaganda of Bible study than Mr. Richardson's little volume, entitled *Bible Reading in Many Lands*, in which the story of the work of twenty-two years in St. Benet's, Mile End, is so happily told.

The stranger who should choose the morning of Sunday for a visit to St. Benet's Church will find that its congregation, like those of nearly all the churches and chapels around, suffers considerably from the late hours of the Saturday night. On the other hand, as is so generally the case in East London, the value of the Sunday school, in introducing and maintaining earlier hours of rising in many homes, is strikingly obvious. It is indeed a source of great thankfulness and a promise of still better things.

The Wesleyan East End Mission has an important station in the Mile End Road. This is none other than the large and beautiful building known as the Lycett Memorial Chapel. It is now wholly devoted to the purposes of the mission, as are also Stepney Temple and the large chapel in Cable Street, St. George's. No visitor can pass through Mile End without having his attention arrested by the Lycett Chapel and its invitations to the Sunday and other mission services of which it is now the centre. The veteran superintendent of the East End Wesleyan Mission, the Rev. Peter Thompson, not seldom preaches here. We shall hereafter have occasion to notice the labours of this mission not only in Mile End, but in the far poorer and more degraded regions of St. George's, Ratcliff, where perhaps its most notable results are seen. Its work in Mile End is felt to be a great aid to the cause of religion, not only in relation to pre-existing agencies, but in occupying new ground with the methods for which Wesleyanism is so happily distinguished in the cause of evangelisation and revival.

Close by the Lycett Memorial Chapel is Latimer Chapel, the headquarters of a well-known East End mission, conducted for nearly thirty years by the Rev. W. J. Atkinson. Here, in the company of a city missionary attached to the chapel and familiar with the inner life of the district, we may traverse some of the byways of Mile End and learn something of the background of a scene upon which the churches, chapels, and mission halls are throwing a much-needed light. Here we are off the grand and busy highway. Here and there—but not often—we come across an unlovely and sordid street, where the people are half hostile to strangers ; streets where families abound, but homes, alas ! are few, so unattainable in these human warrens seem the ideals of wifehood and motherhood. Happily, the number of such streets has rapidly diminished of late years. But let us ask our guide to speak for himself.

'Does your experience,' we inquire, 'corroborate the views of the vicar of St. Benet's as to the social and religious progress of Mile End ?'

'Speaking generally,' replied our guide, 'yes ! In spite of certain bad survivals of the old slum areas, there is a very visible and great improvement throughout the district. The work of the city missionary and the district visitor has been made easier.

'Fifteen or twenty years since,' continued our informant, 'there was an extent and mass of slum area almost impregnable to visitation—you may see some of it now in the older by-streets near the Assembly Hall and the Globe Road, and between the Lycett and Latimer Chapels. Of late years, the district has shared the general progress of East London in the matter of new buildings and rehousing of the population. The wide-spreading slum settlements and rookeries no longer hold together ; they have been broken up by the newer social and commercial movements and enterprise — by magnificent Board schools, by railway extension, by model dwellings, and by a greatly improved civic administration. A bird's-eye view from one of our overhead railway stations would astonish you with the sight of new towers and spires and lofty roofs stretching far away to Bethnal Green and beyond.'

Here we may add that Mile End Old Town as a whole compares very favourably with Whitechapel, Spitalfields, and St. George's—not to speak of the great towns in the Midlands and the North—as regards its general habitable conditions, and a visit serves to dispel much of the exaggeration of which East London is too often the subject. Mr. Charles Booth (*Labour and Life of the People*) remarks that Mile End Old Town looks very clean and new, in spite of its name. Its streets, even the narrowest, look comparatively wide; the air is fresh, and the squares and other small open spaces are frequent. He adds: 'Altogether it is much the least poverty-stricken of East End districts.'

'And yet,' we remark, 'your work amongst the poor, the vicious, and the outcast still remains?'

'Yes, but with a difference. Remember, it is London we are talking of—East London, a huge population, living on precarious industries, and their lives spent in material cares. We have in Mile End no great settled industries for skilled workers, except perhaps the three great breweries in the Mile End Road, which employ some thousands of men. The proportion of women workers, single and married, young and old, who keep the home together by getting needlework from the wholesale houses is very large, and they are among the very worthiest of the population.'

'The personal visitation of the poor, then,' we remarked, 'is not a declining branch of church work? The mission halls on Sundays and other days are not taking its place?'

'Certainly not; on the contrary, district visiting is decidedly rising in the scale of church agencies. Under the improved conditions I have described, homes for the virtuous and godly poor are now possible in districts which were once wholly vile; but the struggle for a livelihood is very hard, and personal visitation is obligatory as ever, if we are to cheer and aid God's poor.'

Such are some of the lessons which are taught during a Sunday at Mile End. It is not given to us fully to interpret the varied social phenomena we have so briefly sketched. East London, in its vast complexity, is beyond the grasp of even the most qualified of Christian sociologists. But unmistakably the religious awakening which finds expression in the mission agencies already glanced at will be a matter of thankfulness and delight to every visitor.

On the other hand, there are serious phases of an apparently transition period which are far more difficult to read. Chief amongst them is the increasing overflow of the Jewish population from Whitechapel into Mile End, accompanied as it is by a displacement of the Gentile residents, which narrows the area of Christian work. But the diminution of the Gentile population has been accompanied with an increasing diffusion of religious light and life in the homes of the poor. There is abundant reason to believe that the influence of the churches in their several localities would be grievously misjudged by taking the Sunday congregations as the standard. Social contrasts, it has been often and truly said, are keenly felt by the East End struggling poor, many of whom naturally avoid comparison with their better-dressed neighbours at church or chapel; and hence perhaps a still further extension of the outside work of the churches, and an increase of the humbler centres of religious life, may be looked for in the future. Great social changes are unmistakably in progress; but a stranger will find it impossible to spend a Sunday in East London and not see how largely the better life of the community is still, humanly speaking, in the hands of the churches.

VIII

BOW AND BROMLEY

BEYOND populous Mile End and the once rural Tower Hamlets, where farmhouses stood in the last century, we start on another Sunday morning to penetrate still farther eastward and gain a glimpse of the newer world which London is making for itself upon the Essex border. The densely peopled and busy settlements of Bow and Bromley await us ; and almost before we know it, we are within the borders of a new municipality of some two hundred and fifty thousand souls.

Bow and Bromley, rural within living memory, have long since been engulfed in the great metropolis. Here, as in Mile End and Stepney, we shall see some of the signs of the teeming life of the docks and the river-side, but more of the industries of a huge inland city. It seems impossible in East London to get wholly away from seaport industries, and the signs of the hard lot of chronic vicissitude which are the sad heritage of unskilled and casual labour. A Sunday spent in such scenes will happily introduce us to new and abounding and gracious ministries as well as to new needs, ministries which bless alike him that gives and him that takes.

Our destination is the mission field of Harley House, Bow. Harley House, it hardly needs to be said, is a household word in Bow and Bromley and the regions beyond. Its rise and growth during the last twenty years, and the position it now holds among the mission agencies of the metropolis, are a remarkable feature of the religious life of our time. The far-reaching work

BOW CHURCH

of Harley House in the field of foreign missions does not come within the scope of a book on Sunday in East London. Yet, as we walk Bow Common or the purlieus of the docks with the Harley House student-missionary or deaconess, we shall feel the spell and inspiration of the larger sphere. At the back of the home mission will be easily seen the enthusiasm which started the Livingstone Mission of 1878, and to-day sustains single-handed the Congo-Balolo Mission in West Africa, and has since the year 1872 sent out 760 evangelical labourers all over the world.

The approach to Bow from the West End and the Bank is along the great eastern highway which our readers have already traversed. After passing the East London Tabernacle in Burdett Road, easily visible from the great main thoroughfare, Bow Church is less than a mile in front of us. Before we reach that venerable sanctuary, with its fine old trees, and its great time-piece high up in the central tower, standing in the middle of the busy thoroughfare, we notice on the left the Harley House group of houses. Bow Road is one of London's pleasant and almost stately suburban avenues, a fine spacious and leafy boulevard with large and lofty houses on either side.

Here, then, is Harley House. In the spacious grounds behind is Harley College. On the opposite side of the Bow Road, exactly fronting Harley House, is Doric College, the Women's and Deaconesses' branch of the Institute. In Tomlin's Grove hard by is the Deaconesses' Nursing Home ; in High Street, Bromley, is Harley Hall (the centre of Harley House Medical Mission) ; and a mile farther, in Bromley-by-Bow, anybody will direct us to Berger Hall, the headquarters of Harley House East London mission work.

Harley House has been admirably chosen and equipped as a centre for its many agencies. In its various buildings, the men and women gather week by week, the deaconesses in their dark blue uniforms and bonnets coming over from Doric Lodge for certain classes, and the men living and working on the spot. The spacious grounds are used in the summer as an open-air reception room for the many beneficiaries of the mission in Bow

and Bromley. All through the days of a hot July, we should
see detachment after detachment of friends and poorer neighbours entertained at tea in the spacious marquee—the men of
the Bible class, the factory girls, the lads of the night school,
four or five hundred infants, the women from the mothers'
meetings and mission hall, and the policemen and postmen of
the district.

Sunday is a busy day at Harley House. Some of the student-

HARLEY HOUSE

missionaries go forth and give their aid to the churches and
chapels around, in teaching, preaching, or visiting ; others visit
the sailors at the docks and hold services in lodging-houses and
mission halls.

A visit to the docks, in company with one of the Harley
House workers, shows in a striking manner the value of the
foreign languages acquired at the College for mission purposes.
As we stand at the dock gates or on the quays, or stop to interview a foreign sailor in the street, our companion is able to

speak in their own tongue to the Lascars, the Hindu coolies, or the Japanese seamen ; to inquire about their lodgings, and direct or take them to safe and suitable quarters, and to give them Testaments and tracts in their own language. Another missionary, equally well equipped with the languages of Northern Europe, converses with Swedish, Norwegian, Russian, Danish, or German sailors to the same good end. Every Sunday sees a band of Harley House student-missionaries endowed with 'the gift of tongues' start forth on this beneficent errand.

In order further to reach the foreign sailors, the lodging-houses

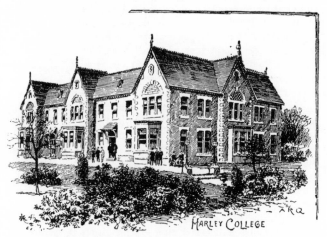

HARLEY COLLEGE

and gathering-places in the neighbourhood of the following docks are visited : East London, West India, South-West India, Limehouse Basin, and the Albert and London Docks. The scope of the linguistic training at Harley College and branches may be inferred from the fact that as many as fifteen different languages were represented among the students last year.

Nor are the deaconesses less fully occupied in local evangelistic work. They teach in half a dozen Sunday schools, visit the sick on Bow Common, conduct classes at Berger Hall, address the children at Dr. Barnardo's Iron Hall, Edinburgh Castle ;

speak at the Mile End Women's Shelter, hold the Harley Hall
Mothers' Bible class and young women's meetings, and conduct
a senior school for the match-girls and matchbox makers of Bow
Common.

'The old stairway at Doric Lodge,' writes Miss Lucy Guinness,
'is trodden by forty young sisters, whose loving, gentle lives
make our deaconesses' branch, as one of its inmates said, one of
the "happiest homes in London." As we wait, they go up to the
little cubicle bedrooms fitted away between narrow wooden
partitions, and come down in dark blue cloaks and bonnets ready
equipped for their afternoon or evening mission away on Bow
Common or Bromley-by-Bow. Night by night they wend their
way, sometimes a group together, sometimes a pair of fast friends,
down Bow Road, past Bow Church, with its big neighbouring
"publics," and down High Street, Bromley, to our mission halls.
And may God bless them as they go!'

In the summer evenings they conduct small open-air meetings
in out-of-the-way courts, where mothers stand at their doors
with babies in their arms. In the winter they hold cottage
meetings. The all-important medical mission carried on by the
deaconesses does not come specially before the visitor on Sundays,
but we shall get a glimpse of it if we call in at Berger Hall.

Let us visit one of the special mission-fields to which the
deaconesses are devoted. Our destination is one of those comparatively newly-settled districts where rural houses still
survive, amidst most unrural surroundings. Such is Bow
Common, as it is still called, although for nearly thirty years it
has had a thickly-settled and poor population.

Starting from Harley House, we get another sight of well-to-
do Bow on our route. Bow Road, the great promenade on
Sundays and holidays, wears its Sunday aspect ; it is alive with
the well-dressed and the well-to-do. The well-laden tram-cars
and omnibuses are going eastward to Bow Bridge and Stratford,
and the Greater London which overflows into Essex. Just before
we reach the North London railway station and the Bow and
Bromley Institute, we leave the great main road and turn to the
right.

A walk of half a mile brings us to an open and bleak district of treeless streets and miles of small two-storied tenements. Here dwell the workers and the workless, who settle in tens of thousands on the skirts of London's arterial thoroughfares.

The part to which we have penetrated is the well-known quarter of the matchbox makers. Here they share Bow Common with the great *cheffonier* industries whose wharves and quays back on to the Limehouse Canal, and occupy many acres of ground. Beside them are chemical works, furnaces, tall chimney stacks, and the timber wharf of Messrs. Byrant & May, the lucifer match manufacturers. Here, in the by-streets, and in the chief thoroughfare, in many a house, and in some streets in nearly every room, we shall find the workers in the matchbox industry. Bow Street, Gale Street, Furze Street, Perring Street, and Weston Street know them well. Some of the girls are standing at the doors, and they hail our guide with a smile and a word as we pass. We shall see them again shortly at Berger Hall, for they are members of the Factory Girls' Union Bible Class.

This is Devon's Road, of which we have heard so much in East London mission literature. To the credit of Bow, be it said, it is the centre of a surprising amount of religious effort. Here is Somerset Hall, a branch of the Factory Girls' Union. Here, too, the Rev. Archibald Brown and his congregation at the East London Tabernacle are in possession : they are the owners and managers of the fine pile of dwellings known as Christian Buildings, where the decent and godly poor are housed in comfortable and sanitary quarters at a cheap rate. All Hallows Church, the great church of Bow Common, is also here served by hard-working clergy.

Children abound in every street. Happily, every few yards we are confronted with the signs of noble efforts on a large scale to bring them under training. At Blackthorn Street Chapel there are 800 children in the Sunday school, and 400 of the drift children in addition are under instruction and visitation. The Wesleyan Church and schools are also doing important work for the children. A few yards farther, in Bow Common Lane, we come upon the magnificent Roman Catholic church, just erected at a cost of £20,000, with spacious and lofty schools attended by 500 children daily. Exactly opposite is the great Board school filled with 1200 children, many of whom have no shoes or stockings.

Altogether it would not be too much to say that the churches, chapels, and mission halls in and about Devon's Road outnumber the public-houses—a notable and creditable fact in this densely settled quarter.

The general aspect of the people is sufficient to account for the number of mission agencies. The match-making population are intermixed with and indeed largely outnumbered by a less fortunate class, in which the unskilled, the casuals, and the chronic ' out-o'-works ' figure very largely. The women with shawls over their heads remind us of the poorer parts of Manchester, Warrington, Preston, and Leeds. Probably the custom was introduced from the North. Only here and there in the very poorest parts of London does the shawl take the place of the bonnet or other headgear. Groups of factory and work girls stand at the street corners, feathers and fringes blowing round their rough, good-natured faces.

' And these are the quarters of the match-girls and matchbox makers ? ' we ask. ' Are they a large population ? '

' Yes, these are some of the girls who work at Bryant & May's, at Bell's, Palmer's, and other match factories. There are six or seven large manufactories at the East End. The industry employs some thousands of hands, girls and women together ; the Fairfield Works alone employ twelve hundred. Next comes Bell's, where some six hundred are employed. Of course all the workers do not reside on Bow Common ; the match industry attracts girls for a couple of miles round, but I know no other spot like this as a centre for match-girls and matchbox makers.'

' And the work of the deaconesses from Doric Lodge lies a good deal amongst this class ? ' we ask.

' Yes ; our mission at the hall has a special department for the factory girls. Our medical mission to the houses of the district and general visitations give us a large acquaintance with them.'

' You feel that as a class they have a special claim on you ? '

'Oh yes ; look at their surroundings ! Matters have, of course, greatly improved during the last ten years, but who can visit this part of Bow Common without a chill at the heart ? It is not so much a question of poverty as of a better social atmosphere, and the means to a brighter and better life. Even their better wages are often a source of danger. Earning nine or ten shillings a week, a girl is much tempted to break away from home and set up for herself, and she often does so, renting a room or sharing it with a fellow-worker. Who can wonder if the music halls in the Bow Road and Mile End become their favourite resorts ?'

'What is the character of the girls as a whole ?' we asked.

'Well, it has been roughly but pretty accurately summed up by an East End police magistrate, who knew the match-girls exceedingly well, and took great interest in them. Mr. Montagu Williams said : "Taking the class as a whole, they well repay any genuine interest shown in their welfare. Most of them are eager to marry, and they do so very young. Many a match-girl of sixteen marries a dock labourer or factory hand who is no older. Their happiness is of short duration. Very often one of these poor creatures, a month or two after marriage, applies to me for protection against her husband, and frequently when I have heard the case I could not help admitting that the husband had a great deal to complain of. He has very likely worked hard and never failed to take home his earnings to his 'missis,' as he calls her ; and yet, night after night, he has returned to a dirty and neglected fireside, and found no dinner and no wife awaiting him. Still," the magistrate continued, "the marriages of the match-girls do sometimes turn out well."'

Alas, that the early life of a match-girl should afford so little opportunity for domestic training ! But the children of the outworkers, the matchbox makers, are in perhaps a still worse position. They are set to work with knife and paste the moment they return from the Board school. They have no play, and very little time to rest. At early dawn the 'skillets,' as the bundles of wood are called, are brought out, and the whole family is soon at work.

Such, then, is a glimpse of the world in which the deaconesses of Doric House visit day after day as physicians of both body and soul. Happy indeed is it for many a girl and many a family in Bow Common and down in Bromley that from the Harley House and Doric Lodge point of view the medical mission is an indispensable accompaniment of the deaconesses' work, especially when wifehood and motherhood and the ties of family life have taught the match-girl the worth of friendship and sisterly help.

Berger Hall is in Bromley, half a mile or more from the scenes we have just witnessed. It is a large building, an old-time chapel upon which newer buildings have been grafted. The district is poor, and here and there squalid. Like other centres of casual labour, it reminds the visitor of the saying that 'East London largely consists of those who are about to leave it, or those who have failed to leave it.' It is nevertheless a mixed population, and the godly and self-respecting poor are interspersed here, as in other parts of needy East London. The 'solidarity of slumland,' as it was called, is now almost a thing of the past, notwithstanding that shawl-headed mothers and bare-headed children are grouped about the streets. The site has been well chosen by the Harley House authorities as the centre of its East London mission hall.

Sunday is a busy day at Berger Hall. This morning no less than nine hundred of the children of the streets and courts around have been assembled, as usual, at the Sunday school : nearly the same number will meet in the evening at a bright and pleasant service. These children are in many cases nicely dressed for the occasion, showing that Berger Hall is appreciated by the better-class industrial poor, who maintain their self-respect, and the Sunday habits they had perhaps learned in better days and in less unfavourable surroundings.

Passing the minor hall and the various classrooms, we are taken upstairs to one of the sights we are specially in search of. This is the senior class for factory girls already mentioned. (Just outside the hall is Bell's great match factory.) A happier Sunday afternoon scene could certainly not be witnessed in Bow. A deaconess from Doric House is in charge, as usual. A hymn is being sung, and the bright, strong voices of the girls remind us of the singing of their industrial sisters, the mill-hands of the North of England, at the afternoon Sunday school. Prayer by the deaconess is followed by the Scripture study for the day. The manner of the girls shows how thoroughly their teacher has their confidence, and we learn afterwards how closely Doric Lodge keeps in touch with them during the working week. They are of the age when so many of their fellow-workers 'set up for themselves,' as already described.

On the mantelshelf of the room a placard of a missionary character attracts our attention. It tells of the departure of the former deaconess in charge of the school to undertake mission work at the Congo-Balolo district in West Africa, and from it we learn that the match-girls contribute regularly and substantially to her support, looking upon her as their special representative in the Dark Continent.

If we cross the Bow Road and enter Fairfield Road, we shall find a group of buildings devoted solely to the interests of the match-girls and factory workers. This is none other than the Clifden House Institute. It consists of four houses, and a large dining-hall built out at the back, and there are dormitories for a certain number of the girls. The site has been well chosen, for Messrs. Bryant & May's lofty and handsome range of factory buildings is just opposite. The Institute was founded in 1889 by the Viscountess Clifden, assisted by Lady Sarah Spencer and other friends interested in the working-girls of East London. Here on Sunday evenings we shall always find a congregation of factory girls assembled to a service conducted by one of the missionaries from Harley House.

The week-day uses of the Institute to the girls and women are manifold, and give the girls the home-training and knowledge of needlework and cooking which in many cases would otherwise not be obtained at all. The employers, who contribute liberally, gladly remark upon the notable improvement in the general character of the girls and women brought under the influence of Miss Nash, the superintendent, and her staff of Christian workers at the Institute.

In the immediate neighbourhood there are many hundreds of working-girls for whom, at present, Clifden House has no accommodation, a fact which will be readily understood when it is remembered that the great factory over the way alone employs twelve hundred female workers. So humane and Christian an enterprise should commend itself to all who are interested in the progress of the people. The management is vested by Lady

CLIFDEN HOUSE
INSTITUTE

Clifden in the Factory Helpers' Union, whose main object is 'to promote the moral and spiritual welfare of factory and working girls, and to lead them to the knowledge of the Lord Jesus Christ as their Saviour.'

But we must return to Berger Hall. We have yet to see the room in which some two hundred of the drift children are gathered every Sunday. These little ones are less accustomed to Sunday services or gatherings of a religious kind than the regular attendants at the Hall. Accordingly, a somewhat freer and less formal service is provided for them. Its peculiarity is that it is entirely conducted by teachers of their own class in life, young men and women who have been rescued from irreligion and gradually trained into usefulness.

Last, but by no means least, is the service for adults on Sunday night, conducted by the able and estimable missionary, Mr. Heywood. This is attended by some eight hundred men and women. Here again the deaconesses from Doric Lodge render invaluable service. Thus, on Sundays the Hall with its many resources and its admirable equipment of zealous agents is fully utilised.

Berger Hall has a room devoted to the Harley House Medical Mission. In our walk through the highways and byways of Bow Common we have seen more than enough to understand the value of such a mission. We stand in the dispensing room, in front of long rows of glass bottles, jars, and drugs ; and we are told something of the high-class medical training and qualifications of the deaconesses, or the 'lady doctors,' as the people call them. Miss Rees, who undertakes the management of the medical mission, and has proved herself a gifted, devoted, and loving worker in this trying sphere, says that seventeen deaconesses have passed the examination of the London Obstetrical Society, and twenty-six have received the professional nurse's training. Of course the work of the nursing branch— on Sundays as well as other days—is very trying. Many of the houses attended are three or four miles distant from each other, and six or seven hours are sometimes needed for one case. The centre of the Medical Mission is at Harley Hall, High Street, Bromley.

The work has become known by degrees. More than 5000 medical visits have been paid since the work began in 1889. During the last two years, 5232 visits have been paid.

The people appreciate these, and 'the ladies' of Tomlin's Grove (the Nursing Branch) have become popular. They are known by numerous appellations, from the 'lady doctors' to the 'Guinness girls.' 'Angel of light' is one of the titles bestowed upon Miss Rees.

'There are very few departments of home mission work,' remarks Miss Lucy Guinness, 'which make more severe demands for patient sympathy and Christ-like service than that which the Doric Lodge deaconesses have made their life-calling. Only those who know the narrow dirty quarters which the East London poor call "home," who have visited the crowded single rooms in which whole families live, eat, sleep, work, and often hold drunken quarrels ; who have sat by sufferers in the tainted atmosphere of court and alley sickrooms ; only they can understand what it is to stand hour after hour in such unflinching yet consecrated service.'

'Send us a *Hakim* in the likeness of Christ,' was the appeal once addressed to Mrs. Bird-Bishop by the chieftain of a nomad tribe on the waste steppes of Turkistan. 'It was a plea,' this lady writes, 'for a Christian doctor, a medical missionary. The man or woman most in the likeness of Christ is the one most needed. His life will be a living epistle.' Nothing less than this ideal of character and service in the waste steppes of East London is sufficient for the work of Miss Rees and her sister workers at Doric Lodge.

A Sunday at Bow will also show us some of the more prosperous and older centres of church work. The sight will be a welcome one, after the scenes we have witnessed. In these respects, the Bow of a former generation is still happily represented ; and the work of the past, in church and chapel alike, remains unsubmerged by the newer tide which flows around it in ever increasing volume. The handsome and substantially built places of worship in the Bow Road, still holding their own in changeful times, and the large houses and mansions of the older suburban type, still standing in their spacious gardens, tell of the continuity of the older life.[1] But even here the signs of

---

[1] In the letters of one recently passed away, written when he was a youth with a doctor at Bow, he is found saying how delightful it was to live in such a quiet country village, and telling of his walks, and the birds and the flowers. How great the change to-day ! Metropolitan problems will never be solved if the suburban areas are not brought under view before the population settles upon them.

past prosperity are gradually fading. The well-to-do citizens and sea-captains of the port of London who once made Bow their home have now gone farther east for the countryside, and are being fast supplanted by a poorer population. Still, as we shall see, life is not lived wholly on the lower levels in Bow.

The East London Tabernacle is the home of one of the most notable religious organisations of Bow. It is here that Mr. Archibald Brown, who is at East London what the late Mr. Spurgeon was at South London, carries on his public ministry. The building is situate at the western margin of the parish, as Bow Church is at the east. It abuts upon Mile End, being within a few minutes' walk of the Peeple's Palace.

It is Sunday morning, and streams of well-dressed people are setting in from all quarters—from Mile End, Stepney, and Bow —towards the Tabernacle. Soon the spacious building, with its wide floor and capacious galleries, is well filled. The scene is unparalleled in this part of the metropolis. Morning congregations in East London are almost everywhere at a minimum ; yet here every Sunday is gathered, for the eleven o'clock service, a congregation of nearly two thousand persons.

The service is marked by a simplicity which takes us back to the public worship of a former generation. In the musical portion, chanting is unknown, and there is no organ to accompany the singing. The hymns are sung with impressive congregational fervour, and each verse is read out by the minister before it is taken up by the congregation. A Bible is in the hands of almost every one of the congregation, and is frequently required for reference during the sermon.

Of the gifted preacher and pastor who has ministered here for nearly thirty years, nothing need be said ; but the impression made upon the stranger as the sermon takes hold of the vast congregation is not easily forgotten. The sight throws a new and unexpected light upon life at Bow. The revelation it affords of the forces which are here at work on behalf of the East London Sunday, and all it imports for the huge population around, may well awaken the deepest thankfulness.

But, alas, here, as at the Great Assembly Hall in Mile End Road, there is another and a perplexing aspect of the scene. The congregation, here as there, imposing as it is in its numbers, is disappointing as regards the classes of the population represented. Here, as at Mile End, we miss those whose attendance is doubtless most coveted, though not obtained—the labouring poor and casuals, who form nearly three-fourths of the industrial population around. Needless to say to those who are familiar with East London, it is no new discovery which thus troubles the visitor; nor indeed is the problem it suggests peculiar to any one congregation or denomination. More or less we find it everywhere present in our Sunday observation of East London. What, then, it may be asked, in the instance before us, is the view which is taken of the facts by the preacher and pastor himself, who knows so well the social condition of the people among whom he labours?

Some notes of an interview with the Rev. Archibald Brown may well help us in the inquiry. It may, perchance, tell us how far the church-going and non-church-going habits of the district are a reflection of the religious condition of the poorer population around.

'Your congregation,' we ventured to remark to Mr. Archibald Brown, 'is a well-to-do congregation for such a district?'

'Yes,' was the reply, 'it is a well-to-do, liberal, and generous congregation, and I have much to be thankful for. But you must not take it as representing the district around the Tabernacle, or even as a Bow congregation.'

'It is not, then, a local congregation?'

'Oh no!' replied Mr. Brown; 'those days have long since gone by. They come from far and wide, from the more rural districts farther east, from Woodford and other parts of Essex, from over the Hertfordshire borders and other comparatively distant places, where so many of our Bow people have migrated since Bow and Bromley have "gone down."

'You will be surprised,' Mr. Brown went on to say, 'to hear that out of seventeen hundred of our church members thirteen hundred live away from Bow.

'When I came here, nearly thirty years ago,' Mr. Brown

continued, 'Bow was a villa suburb, and the churches and chapels were in a fair proportion to the population, and, humanly speaking, equal to the claims made upon them. To-day, the well-to-do have fled, and we are flooded with a poor population out of all proportion to our means for dealing with them.'

'And this new population,' we asked, 'do not come to church or chapel—not even to the East London Tabernacle?'

'No; it is useless to expect it, at least so far as the Tabernacle is concerned; the two classes will not blend—the very poor and

EAST LONDON TABERNACLE

the well-to-do. If the former are not found at the Great Assembly Hall, where the congregation is perhaps two or three grades lower than my own, how can we expect them here?

'But,' continued Mr. Brown, 'for all that, don't infer that our poor—for so I look upon them—at Bow Common and elsewhere are not shepherded. Far from it, as my missionaries will show you, if you have a morning to spare. No; our poor are the greatest charge on our time and our means. Speaking for myself, grateful as I am for my Sunday congregations, and much as I delight in my ministrations to them, I perhaps prize still more our daily mission work amongst God's poor.'

Mr. Brown went on to express his regret at the class divisions to which he had alluded, but he said he saw no help for it. He accepted the fact and adapted his church work to it.

'In what way,' we asked, 'do you seek to meet it?'

'Partly by planting out mission stations, at which our poor can attend on Sunday. Visit our four mission halls on the Sunday and see for yourself : they are not large, but they are centres of great blessing to the neighbourhood. Even thus it is difficult to form in the people the habit of attending service on the Sunday. But it is the personal visitation of our missionaries day by day throughout the week on which we most rely for evangelisation. This is our most direct means under God of saving souls.'

'And is this part of East London—Bow Common, and the vicinity—improving, as the vicar of St. Benet's says of Mile End, or getting worse? You can speak from nearly thirty years' experience.'

'Decidedly it is improving,' said Mr. Brown, with much earnestness. 'Bow, as it used to be when I first knew it, has gone down almost out of all recognition ; but the worst is over, so far as regards the physical and moral degradation. Matters have universally improved, even during the last few years, and are still improving. The poor here are often badly traduced, and their social condition, bad as it is comparatively, is grossly exaggerated.

'There is indifference to religion,' continued Mr. Brown, 'on a great scale, as your Sunday visits will have shown you, and yet even in this respect things are greatly improving. It is almost impossible to find a street in which there are not godly families, and in the most abject and hopeless-looking places there are solitary Christians shining like stars. In fact, the improvement in Bow, as a whole, often startles me when I look back some fifteen years, to the time of the " Bitter Cry." '

Coming back to our special subject, Sunday in East London, as illustrated at Bow, we find Mr. Archibald Brown had reserved until the last the revelation of one of his most prolific helps to congregational life and Sunday public worship. This is the Saturday-night devotional meeting, which is one of the greatest of occasions at the East London Tabernacle. It is held every week, and is attended by fully one thousand persons. Mr. Brown attaches the greatest importance to this meeting, not only for its immediate object, but also for its bearing on the Sunday services and the Sunday attendance.

Visits to other well-established centres of church life and work in Bow, especially in companionship of the hard-working clergy of the various churches, would well reward the visitor interested in the East London Sunday and the religious condition of the mass of the population. We are concerned in these pages not so much with regular and organised work, as with the characteristic features of life among the people. Any more adequate survey of a more extended nature is beyond our scope, or we might gladly refer to the work of the Harley Road Mission, so long conducted by the Rev. Evans Hurndall, and to similar Christian enterprises of lesser magnitude. Mr. Hurndall's Sunday afternoon addresses at Bow Institute were attended by no less than fifteen hundred people. His work was indeed many-sided, but his Men's Own Meeting afforded a notable illustration of what is still possible in directions where many despair. It must be matter of general satisfaction that his successor has a like passion for work among the masses of the people.

Thus, in the great and less-known background of the million-peopled East, we have learned again not only more of the wants of an ever-widening human world, but more of the influence which sorrow and suffering can exert to bring Christ-like workers from far and near to solace and save the needy and 'him that is ready to perish.'

IX

STEPNEY

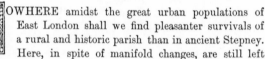OWHERE amidst the great urban populations of East London shall we find pleasanter survivals of a rural and historic parish than in ancient Stepney. Here, in spite of manifold changes, are still left some of the green open spaces and memorable houses of former days, whose kindred have almost wholly disappeared from the parishes around. Stepney Green and Stepney Church and churchyard would alone suffice to give the parish the first place in East London's memorials of the historic and the picturesque.

Stepney Green, with its red-brick houses of the time of Queen Anne and the Georges, conspicuous by their large palisaded forecourts, quaint porches, and deep windows, would alone reward a visit. The venerable and village-like parish church of St. Dunstan, with its grey tower and battlements, surrounded by its wide-spreading and leafy 'God's Acre,' remains much as it was in mediæval times, and wears its weight of years with unchanging grace and beauty.

Stepney is the centre of the local parochial system. In the best days of Stepney Green, when it was the favourite home of London's most prosperous citizens and of titled families, Stepney parish extended from the City and Spitalfields down to the marshes of Blackwall. It was the mother parish of all that we now call East London.

In order to reach Stepney from the City or the West End, we shall again make our way to familiar Aldgate and Whitechapel. Thence we may proceed down the Mile End Road until we find

Stepney Green lying just off the highway—opposite Charrington's
Brewery, and near the Great Assembly Hall.   Or we may choose
a parallel route from Aldgate—the Commercial Road, another
of the grand thoroughfares which run from Whitechapel eastward.

In the Commercial Road, East London is seen in its older
and less attractive commercial aspects.   Yet, as we traverse its

OLD MANSIONS
STEPNEY GREEN

unlovely length, flanked with great townships on either side,
we get glimpses of better things.   Off the main thoroughfare,
and amidst the populous byways, it is difficult to get out of
sight of church, chapel, or lofty Board school.

Let us note some of these beacons as we go.   In Settle Street,
on our right hand, is the fine new church dedicated to St.
Augustine.   The parish is memorable for the work done in it
by the late Edward Denison.   His untimely death, like that of

Toynbee and Keith Falconer, is still fresh in the minds of East Londoners. The church is supported by the Oxford Christ-church Mission, and here the Rev. Harry Wilson now lives and labours night and day among his poor. There is a special com-munion service held monthly in Hebrew for the Jewish proselytes.

Next we arrive at Philpot Street, where is a famous East London landmark. It is the historic Wycliffe Chapel, founded as far back as 1642, and in the present century linked with the honoured name of its well-known pastor, Dr. Andrew Reed, founder of the Reedham Orphan Asylum. Here, too, the work of Dr. Reuben Thomas is gratefully remembered. Next door is the welcome sight of the newly built Mildmay Central Hall, which is devoted to an evangelical mission to the Jews, combined with a medical mission. St. Philip's, Stepney, is at the end of the street, just at the back of the London Hospital.

Then comes into view one of the unhappiest features of the East End Sunday. This is the notorious Watney Street Sunday market. We hear the cries and clamour of voices before we come upon the busy and unsavoury scene. It is chiefly a food market; the stalls, boards, and barrows, heaped up with fish and meat, green-stuff lying about in heaps, fruit in bulk, and eggs everywhere. It is, we note, a women's market; and the women are the wives of dock-labourers and longshoremen, ill-clad, badly fed, and their hard lives reflected in every feature. Unhappily, too, many of them are one-room occupants, and are thus unable to store food for the morrow's dinner. The high rent charged for dwellings is grievously felt here. Watney Street has an ill-repute for general degradation. The late Mr. Montagu Williams declared it to be worse than Ratcliffe Highway.

In the midst of the market is planted the Ebenezer Mission chapel and mission hall, conducted by the Rev. B. Sackett, and here an ameliorative work has been maintained for many years. Here also is Christchurch, Watney Street, a magnificent building. It provides thirteen hundred seats, all of which are free. Some two or three hundred persons are gathered in at the morning service, but the work, as may be imagined, is not chiefly sanctuary work. The vicar, the Rev. H. C. Dimsdale, and his three curates, live

WATNEY STREET SUNDAY MARKET.

on the spot in a clergy-house close to the footway, where day and night they bear the disturbances with fortitude, and work to win souls.

Passing Stepney Temple, a notable centre of the East End Wesleyan Mission (whose work will come before us in another chapter) we turn into a side-street in search of Stepney Church. Three or four beautifully open and tree-planted squares refresh the eye as we traverse the wilderness of streets (which are themselves wide and well-planned), and remind us how often such pleasant contrasts occur in much-calumniated East London.

We are now in historic Stepney. In most of the streets the houses have arched windows with Gothic mullions, and cotta e shutters outside, folding backwards.

The music of the beautiful bells of the parish church is floating over the housetops, and easily guides us to our destination. At the corner of White Horse Street we pass Colet Place, built on the site of the old house of Dr. Colet, a former vicar of Stepney, Dean of St. Paul's, and founder of St. Paul's School. Every step now takes us farther into historic ground.

Stepney old churchyard is a magnificent survival of village days, some eight acres in extent. The ancient church tower rises above the leafage. On the south it is approached through a long grove of shady sycamores. We are in the heart of East London, yet so rural is the scene we might be at Willesden or Harrow, in front of their kindred church towers and chimes of village bells. Indeed, the rustic days of Stepney are by no means far distant. In the last century Stepney was described in the books and newspapers of the time as 'near London.'

It is eleven o'clock, and we enter by the ancient western porch, and find ourselves in an old English parish church. The most welcome sight is the wide main isle, providing the best seats in the church free for the poor. They are well filled this morning with the humbler parishioners. It is altogether an excellent congregation. There are some six or seven hundred persons present. In the evening, we are told, the church is filled with nearly twice that number.

We shall learn hereafter from the rector himself that it is not the congregation of twenty years since, when middle-class families were more numerous in Stepney; but judging by our recent Sunday visits to adjoining districts there is an unusually strong centre of church life and organisation at Stepney parish church. A beautiful, reverent, and hearty service of prayer and praise confirms the impression made upon the visitor. On this occasion it was followed by a practical, earnest, and suggestive sermon from a stranger, who was preaching for the Rev. E. Hoskyns, the rector.[1]

The parish numbers some 26,000 residents. Mr. Hoskyns is assisted by six curates. The Sunday schools have an average attendance of 1000, and there are 104 teachers. The rector conducts a special Bible class for men on Sunday afternoons, attended by some sixty, who are communicants or about to be confirmed. During his fifteen years at Stepney Mr. Hoskyns has built a mission church—St. Faith's—with mission buildings attached. The day schools take a very high place in his view of church and parish work. They are attended by 1500 children.

In an interview with Mr. Hoskyns, he was kind enough to talk freely on parish matters, and to throw some valuable light on church prospects in Stepney. Indeed, some of the facts he was good enough to lay before us will be generally considered as of a somewhat startling and momentous character.

'You are happily placed as a parish clergyman, in this part of the East End,' we ventured to remark. 'There is so much of old rural and prosperous Stepney still around you, so many pleasant, well-to-do streets of the olden time, and we suppose, a well-to-do population?'

Mr. Hoskyns smiled and shook his head. He replied: 'I wish I could accept your congratulations; but you are mistaken. Appearances are very delusive.'

'Do you mean, then, that Stepney has "gone down,"' we asked, 'like other parts of East London?'

'Stepney,' replied Mr. Hoskyns, 'has entirely changed its

[1] This converstion took place in 1895. Mr. Hoskyns has since left London for an industrial parish in the North of England.

character. It is not the same place. The old population has well-nigh left us. Those streets of comely cottages you noticed are no longer occupied by the sea-captains and mates who once made Stepney their home. Quite a different class are now in possession, several families now living in the same house.'

'Then are the middle class disappearing in Stepney as else-where in East London?'

'Yes, rapidly,' replied Mr. Hoskyns; 'and our church resources are in every way impoverished and crippled in consequence. There are now no local industries, and no resident employers in Stepney living among their workpeople and taking the part of citizens and Christians, as they used. Our only employers of labour are the great brewers, and it is due to them to say they give munificently. Without their aid I hardly see how we could keep up the work of the church in the parish.'

'And this disappearance of the middle class seriously dim-inishes the supply of church workers?'

'Yes, seriously,' replied Mr. Hoskyns. 'We have no longer the women of leisure and capacity to work with us, now that the better-class families have gone away to live on the country-side. The poor are now left on our hands. I have still some valuable lay workers, but prospects are not bright. No; this desertion of Stepney, and indeed of East London generally, by the well-to-do classes is bad for us all—bad for the deserters, bad for the poor, and bad for the church.'

Mr. Hoskyns then proceeded to speak of another danger to church work.

'The Jewish problem,' said Mr. Hoskyns, 'is the problem of all others which overshadows us. It is the most perplexing of all recent developments in East London. We in Stepney are feeling in every direction the pressure of the Jewish invasion— the permanent settlement amongst us of a people of another race and religion. So pushing and energetic are the new-comers that they promise to become in time the dominant race.'

We here mentioned to Mr. Hoskyns that we had already seen the signs of the new era on Stepney Green, where in the oldest and best part are to be seen the new and splendid East London

Synagogue, the Jewish Schools, and the Jewish Working Men's Club.

'Yes,' Mr. Hoskyns continued, 'the Jewish overflow from Whitechapel and Mile End into Stepney brings many difficulties. Here is one, for example.'

Mr. Hoskyns here pointed skywards to a lofty building overlooking his rectory walls. 'That,' he said, 'is a Board school, formerly occupied by seven hundred Christian children. Now there are seven hundred Jewish children in their place. Such is the way in which our own population is being supplanted.'

Mr. Hoskyns seemed to hint that in time he might find himself left as the Christian rector of a Jewish parish, so rapidly was the transformation going on in Stepney.

'And yet,' we urged, 'your church is in full work, its equipment fully maintained, and it keeps in the front rank of busy East London parishes. You have built a mission church during the last two years, and have just added a lecture hall and classrooms, and you have a congregation of one thousand people.'

Mr. Hoskyns said this was quite true, and he trusted the clergy of Stepney were giving a good account of themselves and their charge, grappling as they were with the newer difficulties of these later days. The organisation and equipment of the parish for working and administrative purposes was still maintained at the level of the old and more prosperous times, and, indeed, had been extended during the last few years, and certainly no falling off would be allowed in his hands.

As to the additional burden thrown upon himself by the care of 'those things which are without'—the raising of the large annual income from entirely new sources outside the parish, and amounting to some thousands of pounds a year—the rector of Stepney modestly forbore to speak, yet this is the most serious anxiety which besets the rectors of the great East London parishes to-day.

Thus far our survey has not extended beyond inner Stepney, whose population of some 26,000 lies, as it were, in the shadow of the mother church. Outer Stepney, including the whole of the rural deanery, would introduce us to at least forty-five other churches, with populations of an average of 10,000, but rising as high as 21,000 in the case of St. Leonard's, Bromley, and 18,000 at All Saints, Poplar. Such is the scale of the populations which have compelled the subdivision of old Stepney parish.

Close by Stepney Church is another memorable centre of religious life in Stepney, of less antiquity but almost equally well known during the last two hundred and fifty years. This is Stepney Meeting-House, one of the most historic churches of Nonconformity. Stepney Meeting - House is full of cherished associations, both

OLD STEPNEY MEETING HOUSE
BUILT 1674

in the circumstances of its origin and its record of influential and honoured pastors. From its foundation in the stormy times of Archbishop Laud by Henry Burton, the rector of St. Matthew's, Friday Street, who had been private secretary to the Prince of Wales, down to the days of Dr. Joseph Fletcher and Dr. John Kennedy in the present century, Stepney Meeting-House has had an unbroken history of ministerial and congregational life and service in East London.

To-day we no longer find the quaint-looking old meeting-house, with its tiled roof and dormer windows, in existence. Newer times, an increasing population, and the expansive ministrations of its chief nineteenth-century pastor, Dr. Kennedy, compelled the erection some thirty years since of a larger building, more adapted to modern requirements. Accordingly, in 1863, the old meeting-house of 1674 was taken down to give place to

NEW STEPNEY
MEETING HOUSE

the present handsome Gothic building. The new meeting-house is one of the largest and completest of London Nonconformist places of worship. As we enter its spacious and handsome interior, we are taken back to the more prosperous period at Stepney in the present century, the period of flourishing middle-class congregations. Not only is the newer sanctuary a beautiful temple for public worship and the preaching of the Word; there are attached to it a school-hall, lecture-rooms, and classrooms on a scale unparalleled in any other part of London.

Our visit is on a Sunday afternoon, when one of the newest developments of religious life in East London, and especially in Stepney, is to be seen to considerable advantage. This is the weekly meeting of the Stepney Men's Sunday Union. It is akin to the great meeting held at the same time at Poplar Town Hall, where the rector commonly presides.

The constitution of the Men's Sunday Union is distinctively religious. In the words of the founder, 'It is a brotherhood, on a religious basis, requiring both love to God our Father, and love to man our brother.' The pastor of the church is *ex officio* president.

Some four or five hundred men, mostly skilled workmen, were present, this being an average attendance. On special occasions the number reaches one thousand. The proceedings are introduced with prayer and a hymn. The address on this occasion was given by the Rev. Stephen Barrass, the well-known rector of a city church, who delivered a powerful address against betting and gambling. The complete attention and discriminating applause of the audience spoke well for the tone of feeling which is being cultivated at these very popular and successful gatherings.

So large a congregation entirely of one class and one sex inevitably reflects the changes which have taken place in the district. Stepney is now distinctively the abode of labour. 'The district' (writes a Nonconformist correspondent) 'is a difficult one to work in. Jews hold pretty nearly all the trade of Stepney, and so Stepney Meeting-House now lacks the trades-man and lower middle-class element which usually form the backbone of Congregational churches in poor districts. But there is in this neighbourhood a solid foundation of working-men, largely of the foreman class. To the distinctly slum portion of Stepney the meeting-house does not minister. By means of a Bible woman, the needs of the very poor are often met through a home missionary branch, which has a " compassionate society " in connection with it. During the winter, too, dinners are provided for six hundred poor children a week, and in other ways the church tries to ameliorate the lot of the indigent and suffering.' [1]

The last five years have been singularly eventful in the history of the meeting-house. In 1889, the Rev. G. S. Reaney, Dr. Kennedy's successor, resigned ; and in 1893, Mr. Brooks, who succeeded, also resigned ; but the workers who remain are not insensible to the social change in the district around them, or to the equipment which may be needed for the newer era and the newer claims.

Thus is the Stepney of to-day a meeting-place of the old and the new. Standing this Sunday afternoon at the grave in Stepney Churchyard of William Greenhill, the first minister of Stepney Meeting, and at the same time rector of the parish, we look back some two hundred and fifty years, and then turn to the Stepney of to-day. Happy are they who are nobly putting their hands to the plough in faith and hope that every mountain and hill of difficulty shall be made low !

[1] *The Independent*, April 26, 1894.

X

ST. GEORGE'S EAST AND THE LONDON DOCKS

HE social and religious record of East London during the past twenty-five years, so far as concerns the districts we have already visited, is one of obvious and remarkable progress. The still lengthier period of work and service in this ever-widening field which some of us are able to look back upon, and which transports the writer of these lines to the East London of forty years since, enables us to make comparisons and contrasts of a still more encouraging nature. A new impulse for good has affected even the most unpromising of localities, and the better conditions of life which have been established are such as to give new and larger facilities for evangelical service, and to open up the vista of a still newer and a nobler London.

It still remains for us to deal with places which may perhaps present the old and evil features of East London life in their acutest form. Such a district, in the times to which we have referred, was the ill-famed Ratcliff Highway, in the parish of St. George's East. How will this important part of East London be affected by the verdict we have passed on the East End as a whole?

Ratcliff Highway lives in the history of London as the temporary home of the spendthrift sailor, the headquarters of the crimp, of low dancing-rooms and shameless vice, and of public-houses of a kind hardly known elsewhere. But the locality is not and never has been wholly a region of slums and social degradation. We shall find traces of older London, with its historic associations and better times, here in Ratcliff as well as in Spitalfields, Shoreditch, Stepney, and Bow. Much as there is still to pain and shock the visitor, he will see with pleasure the permanent gifts of the better kind which older London has bequeathed to a poor and much-to-be-pitied population. He will see the magnificent open space attached to the parish church, a beautiful oasis of verdure and shade. He will discover Wellclose Square, where until the year 1868 was the Seamen's Church, whose minister was the famous 'Bo'sun Smith.' Close at hand will be found Prince's Square and the Swedish Church where lies buried beneath the altar the body of Emanuel Swedenborg, the founder of the 'New Jerusalem' Church, by the side of that of Dr. Solander, the companion round the world of Sir Joseph Banks. For many centuries the neighbourhood has had a nautical character. In its worst days its open spaces have been a redeeming feature.

On a summer evening we make our way down the Minories. There are no signs of the citizen Sunday here, as there were in former times, for the busy people of this mercantile thoroughfare are now non-resident. At Great Prescott Street we turn into a well-to-do residential quarter. Here is the well-known Roman Catholic centre of this part of London, the Church of the English Martyrs, noted for its annual procession and open-air commemoration on Tower Hill of its sixteenth-century leaders, who there suffered for their faith. Just opposite to the church, the building of the Jewish Passover Cake Society reminds us that we are still in the region of the Ghetto. So far we are in the midst of a fairly prosperous population.

Emerging into the broad and mercantile Leman Street (where are several large common lodging-houses of the better type) we are nearly at our goal. At the lower end are Cable Street and Dock Street, the two chief portals of St. George's in the East.

In Dock Street, near the border-line of Whitechapel and St. George's East, and close to the chief entrance of the London Docks, is one of the best sights of the East London of the newer era. It is the handsomely rebuilt and enlarged Sailors' Home. It may be called the headquarters of the seamen now arriving in the port of London. It is no new venture, but, as we shall see, its development in recent years is connected with a reformation in the life of the sailor ashore which has hardly any parallel. The building is admirably placed : it is near enough to the docks for business purposes, and also close to the older and more dangerous haunts with which it now successfully competes. It at once attracts the newly-landed seamen to a home of comfort and respectability.

The Sailors' Home is in fact a huge but admirably conducted lodging-house and club, housing comfortably more than four hundred men. Under its roof are four hundred cabins, suitably furnished. In every cabin there is a copy of the Holy Scriptures. There are baths, a large dining-hall and common room, a library, reading-room, bank, bar, and smoking-room. The arrangements for bringing the sailors and their baggage straight from the ship to the Home, so as to save them from the hands of crimps and others who prey upon them, are admirable. At present the Sunday aspect of things will sufficiently reward our attention.

Close to the Sailors' Home, and communicating with it by inner doors, is the Sailors' Church—St. Paul's, Dock Street. It was built in 1847 for the seamen of the port of London. Amongst the most distinguished sailors who took a prominent part in the undertaking were Sir John Franklin, of Arctic fame ; Admiral Parry, Admiral Sir H. Hope, and the Hon. Francis Maude, R.N. The late Prince Consort laid the foundation-stone in 1845, was present at the consecration two years later, and gave the east window and the communion plate.

Let us now enter the Sailors' Home and see the Sunday evening aspect of the place. Groups of well-dressed men are gathered at the doors, as we pass into the large common hall or dining-room. It is difficult to believe that· they are ordinary seamen, so quiet is their speech and so town-like their manner. The bells of the church next door are beginning their inviting peal, and the inner doors leading from the common room to the church are thrown open. Before the men begin to pass through for the evening service, we have time for conversation with one of their number. He is a weather-beaten elderly man, who has

known much of the perils of sea and land alike. He has just
come over with the Australian wool-fleet, whose arrival is
always an important event at the London Docks.

SAILORS' HOME
AND CHURCH.

'Sunday night in London,' we venture to remark, 'is not what
it used to be in your early days. You must have seen great
changes in East London in your time?'

'Yes; I've been backwards and forwards for thirty-five years. London's a different place for us now. It's all altered for the better: you're better lodged, better fed, and better looked after. This Sailors' Home is much better than it was when I first knew it.

'As for Ratcliff Highway,' our informant continued, 'why, nowadays there's hardly a sailor but what scorns to go there. It isn't good enough.'

'The seamen as a class are very much improved?' we remark.

'No class of men have improved more, or think more o' themselves. And so it ought to be! No class o' men have been more looked after the last thirty years.

'No!' he continued. 'We've no call to hang about Ratcliff Highway as we used to do, waiting till the ship's paid off, and kept going by the crimps in drink and pocket-money day after day, till the pay was all owing when we did get it. Sometimes you parted with your kit as well, and you had nothing but what you stood upright in. And all the while perhaps your wife and family were living at another port, expecting you home every day. But all that's altered. At least a man does not have to wait about now for his money, and that's been the saving of us.'

'How did it come about?' we asked.

Our weather-beaten friend replied: 'Look what's going on now! Here's all the wool-fleet men set on shore in the port of London, most of them going to draw their eighteen pounds. Do they hang about and waste their money in Ratcliff Highway? Not a bit of it. The Board of Trade steps in, and alters all that. I landed here yesterday, and I can draw a pound for my fare to Liverpool, where my home is, and have the rest sent on after me. You won't find me here after to-morrow. The same with a hundred more of my mates here. They'll be off to their homes at Cardiff, Hull, Southampton, and other ports, and have their money sent on after them.'

Such was the story told us by one who had gone through the terrors of Ratcliff Highway nearly forty years since. As we took leave of our friend, with congratulations on having lived to see better times, he stopped us with a farewell word.

' Don't go to St. Paul's, Dock Street, to look for all the church-going sailors in London. You'll find them West as well as East. They get to know other parts of London as well as this, and scores of them have gone up from this house to-day to the West End ; others have gone South and North to their own favourite chapels and churches. You would not know 'em, if you saw 'em, they're so well dressed.'

It should be said that there are daily morning and evening prayers at the Sailors' Home, but the managers of the institute, while they openly take godliness as the basis and motive of their work, are careful not to press the inmates with too importunate invitations to take part in religious worship. The services in the mission hall in the building are usually attended by a good many men.

A few hundred yards farther eastward we are in Ratcliff Highway, or St. George's Street East, as it is now called, for the old name of evil savour is repudiated in these better times. Here we shall find other seamen's resorts of the newer kind, which have done so much for the reformation of the district.

The Seamen's Christian Friend Society, with its beautiful and attractive building, stands a conspicuous beacon to the passer-by. If we look in at almost any hour of the day on Sunday, we shall find services, Bible-readings, or school-teaching in progress in the pleasant airy and admirably appointed rooms. There is a Sunday school at 10 A.M., prayer-meeting at 10.30, a service for seamen at 11, and services in German at 4.30 and 7, for the benefit of the many seamen from the German ports. The evening service for English sailors is held at 6.30. Every Sunday evening, before the service, the Gospel Pioneer band, a very competent corps of young men, equipped with brass instruments, sally forth from headquarters to Well Street, where the great boarding - house and home already described form a central gathering-ground for the sailors of this part of town, and hold a bright musical service in the street. They seldom return to the hall in St. George's Street for the indoor worship without some happy captures of stray seamen and unattached loungers, who are made welcome to the homely, hearty, and brotherly service.

SEAMEN'S CHRISTIAN FRIEND SOCIETY.

The large hall here seats five hundred adults. The Scandinavian seamen of the port of London are well looked after by a missionary well accustomed to their language.

It is pleasant to think that this admirable mission, to which the Rev. J. E. Hill has devoted himself for many years, is the direct successor of Bo'sun Smith's mission church in Wellclose Square.

A few hundred yards farther east, skirting the London Docks, we are in the heart of the once infamous and even now pitiful yet admirably missioned Ratcliff Highway. The long and far-stretching thoroughfare is a heart-stirring sight. The population (St. George's is the poorest of East London parishes) have apparently all turned out into the street to get, if it may be, a breath of fresh air this sultry summer evening. It is chiefly a district of one-room families. Men, women, and children have left their close quarters in the courts and alleys around to get into the open street, dusty and arid as it is, for the freedom and change of society out of doors. The street and its company are their chief holiday enjoyments. They prefer the kerbstone and the door-step even to the leafy and spacious church-garden, which, morning and afternoon alike, invites them in vain. The love of trees and grass and sky, which so seldom survives the age of childhood among the very poor, seems to have been pressed out of their hard lives, and to have lacked all chance of growth. The Highway, both here and in the no less populous Cable Street hard by, swarms with groups of women and girls of the poorest class, to whom a head-covering is apparently unknown, save perhaps the shawl owned in partnership with fellow-lodgers. Yet the clean white apron, indicating the presence of an industrial class, and itself a tribute to the Sunday, is very generally worn. The younger people here, as indeed everywhere in London, however untoward the condition of their lives, have the precious gifts of cheerfulness and vivacity.

The men, who are also in social groups, keep their own society. The large number who are well-dressed and quiet in demeanour as they stand together at the doors of humble but respectable lodging-houses, form a remarkably new feature in the district.

The contrast with the Sunday night scenes of twenty-five

years ago is nothing less than startling. In those evil days, and even at a later period, the lowest class of the lawless and the vicious dominated the Highway ; to-day they are a comparatively small and manageable minority. Their old domain is broken up with street improvements and new and sanitary buildings, and settled with an industrial class of residents. Still more noticeable is the multiplication of religious and philanthropic missions. Board schools, reformatory homes, and refuges, whose handsome buildings have taken the place of low dancing-rooms, public-houses, and slums of vice and rowdyism, everywhere greet the eye.

Where, we ask, as we tread again the once familiar footway after many years of absence, where are the fifteen or more dancing saloons for unfortunate seamen and their companions which we once passed in this same thoroughfare in a walk of a few hundred yards? Not a single one remains. We can now pass up and down Ratcliff Highway after three o'clock in the afternoon without molestation, and the sight of a drunkard is a rare occurrence. Both north and south, whole side-streets have disappeared to make decent homes for an honest if extremely poor industrial people.

Ratcliff Highway is undoubtedly much poorer than in the prosperous times of the two great shipping docks—the London Docks and St. Katherine's—which formerly brought many more thousands of seamen annually to its doors. The transfer of shipping business to other parts of the river has made a great difference.

The beautiful music of St. George's church-bells has been all this time floating over the scene we have witnessed. Flanked by the leafy trees and beautiful greensward and flowers of the most spacious churchyard garden we have yet seen in West or East London, the noble and stately parish church stands in conspicuous contrast with the prevailing meanness and sordidness which reign around. In scale and outward magnificence it suggests rather the wealthy and fashionable West End than the purlieus of Ratcliff Highway. Yet we may find it to be more in touch with the population around than appearances suggest.

RATCLIFF HIGHWAY: SUNDAY EVENING.

Evening service has begun. The grand interior has seats for twelve hundred, and some five hundred persons are present. The congregation is indeed much larger and of a more respectable class than might have been anticipated. As we afterwards learn, they are all working-people. The service is bright and musical, and notwithstanding the stately impressiveness of the building both within and without, the people are evidently at home, entering heartily into the service. The rector notes that out of a population of ten thousand, scarcely half a dozen families keep a domestic servant. The days of the well-to-do resident middle-class and local employers of labour in St. George's are over. The furnaces in the great sugar refineries have long been cold, and the last of the employers in this once prosperous and important industry left the parish some years since.

The Sunday-evening congregations in connection with the parish church are to be found elsewhere than at St. George's. There is a very good evening gathering at the sub-parish church of St. Matthew's, Prince's Square. There is a service of a mission character at Tait Street, and another mission hall in St. George's Street. The simpler and shorter services held here are much appreciated by those who are unable to be absent long from home, or who from any cause find the services at the parish church too long.

If we call at the three Sunday schools in the afternoon we shall see them filled with nearly one thousand children. For elder girls, young men, and adult men, poorer girls and mothers, there are five separate Bible classes.

Prebendary Turner, the hard-working rector of St. George's, maintains at considerable cost to himself the full working staff of assistant clergy as it existed in more prosperous times, as also an increased number of parish agencies.

Of the collateral agencies, both civic and social, which are now working for righteousness by removing the grosser scandals and temptations and the inhuman conditions of the older Ratcliff Highway, and indeed the whole of East London, much might be said. Among these may properly be numbered the beautiful open spaces, planted as public gardens, which now so frequently come into view in the very midst of the most sordid-looking and crowded areas. Indeed, St. George's, Ratcliff, has an honourable precedence in the history of these welcome and most gracious features of modern East London. It was here, in the gratefully remembered and oft-cited times of the Rev. Harry Jones's pioneer work as rector, that the open churchyard movement was begun. The successful beautifying of St. George's churchyard and burial-ground soon resulted in one of the most notable of London's open-air beneficences—Lord Meath's Metropolitan Public Gardens Association, whose noble work in Stepney Churchyard we have already seen. The Association's similar work at St. Paul's, Shadwell, and St. James's, Ratcliff (both of which we pass this evening), and a hundred other places, is gradually changing the aspect of London.

So far, then, we have had a preliminary glimpse of life in Ratcliff Highway on Sunday evening, its worse and its brighter side. It remains for us to tell of the more special missions which are supplementing the older established church agencies in St. George's. The melancholy 'Bridge of Sighs,' perhaps the most terrible adjunct of the Ratcliff Highway of the past, with its saddening record of lives prematurely ended in the dark waters below, has long loomed large in the social picture of St. George's ; a Bridge of Hope is slowly but surely rising to take its place.

XI

RATCLIFF HIGHWAY AGAIN

T is now more than eleven years since the East London Wesleyan Methodist Mission was established. Commencing its operations in St. George's Wesleyan Chapel, Cable Street, Ratcliff Highway, the mission is now in possession at the Old Mahogany Bar, formerly a low-class music hall; at Paddy's Goose, once a notorious house on Ratcliff Highway; at Stepney Temple, formerly known as the Seamen's Chapel, in the Commercial Road; and at the Lycett Memorial Chapel in the Mile End Road. The Rev. Peter Thompson has been the superintendent of the mission from the beginning. He has the assistance of two other Wesleyan ministers; of several lay evangelists, and of a sisterhood, whose visits are greatly esteemed in the poor homes of the district.

The so-called Old Mahogany Bar is one of the most remarkable instances of mission work in East London. It is situate in a narrow alley, just at the back of the magnificent Sailors' Home in Dock Street, which we have already described. For many long years it competed but too successfully with its great rival for the possession of the sailor ashore near the London Docks.

The nature and origin of the mission here will be understood from the following incident, as recorded by the Rev. Luke Howard. Four years before the Wesleyan Mission took the premises, Mrs. Reginald Radcliffe and Miss Macpherson were passing through Grace's Alley into Wellclose Square as the evening performances in the music hall were proceeding. The dreadful hubbub that came from the hall startled them. They paused to listen, and were so impressed that they paid the admission fee and went in to see really what could be going on. The sights on the stage and the entire condition of things became so awful to them, that they fell down on their knees together, in the centre of the hall, and in view of the stage and crowd of onlookers, prayed that God would break the power of the devil in the place, and bring the premises into the use of Christian people. Soon after this the place was closed, and the licences lapsed. It was not again opened until February 2, 1888, when it was opened in the name of Christ and for His glory.

The character of the neighbourhood may be further gathered by a glance at Mr. Charles Booth's Map of East London, where this district, notwithstanding the remarkable improvements of later years, is still marked black, as the appropriate colour for the abode of the criminal, semi-criminal, and lawless classes generally.

To-day, a visit on Sunday afternoon or evening will show us an astonishing change. The transformed music hall, which with its galleries holds some six hundred people, is well filled from the courts and alleys around. They form an orderly and attentive congregation of casual workers and out-o'-works, dockers, street-hawkers, irregular workers in small and ill-paid industries, and, alas! those who neither toil nor spin. But the eye also rests upon a large proportion who have been won as regular attendants at a religious service. The closed door up in the gallery, formerly leading to the drinking-bar behind, is the only indication left of the former uses of the building.

Much of the mission work, Mr. Howard tells us, is done among those 'who go down to the sea in ships'; but it must be remembered that apart from the industrial class who may happen to be in or out of employment, the East End is the general 'dumping-ground' for the moral and social débris of the kingdom —wild, harum-scarum lads who run away from home, half-witted ones whom no one cares to employ, profligate prodigals who have spent their substance and have not even pigs to tend, 'broken-downs' and ne'er-do-wells who naturally sink down as the sediments of the great backwaters of London life.

PADDY'S GOOSE.

Add to these the men (no inconsiderable number) who are in adversity through no vice or fault of their own, but who are temporarily edged out of the ranks of the workers by the fierce competition of modern industrialism, and you get a fair representation of a Mahogany Bar Mission congregation.

'And you are seeing some of the result of your labours?' we ask.

'The work is always difficult, but we have abundant encouragement,' is the reply. 'Our labours here must always be chiefly among those whom we cannot retain, the people being always on the move. Yet God's grace is abundantly manifested. We joy in God that so many men and women are won to Him, whether they stay here or go elsewhere.

'A visitor to one or two of our services, especially in the fine summer months, can have but little conception of the varied work carried on at this centre. In connection with the Bar, we have open-air religious services, a flourishing Sunday school— yes, in this very alley which Mr. Booth colours black in his Map —children's meetings, girls' guilds, and the boys' brigade. All sorts and conditions of men are gathered about us, and our ministries among them are as varied as their needs.

'Our medical mission has been an untold boon to numbers of the poorest of the poor. The reclamation of the men is followed up with care and unremitting attention, often leading to their restoration to industry and an honest living as the result of a spiritual change.'

Such is a glimpse of the wonderful work to which the transformed Old Mahogany Bar is now devoted. Naturally enough, the old habitués of the place, who return to it after years of absence to repeat the old carousals, are not a little astonished at the different welcome which now awaits them. Some of them happily are now among the most grateful beneficiaries of the mission.

Farther east—in the heart of Ratcliff Highway—we shall find another outpost of the mission. Here the workers are in possession of the old public-house known far and wide in past years in the sailors' quarters of East London as Paddy's Goose.

The effigy of the goose is still retained outside as in former times, and serves to-day as a beacon for the newer visitors and newer objects. A dancing-room attached to the house made it a favourite centre for the lawless and turbulent as well as the vicious.

Here, then, as at the Mahogany Bar, were found ready to hand premises admirably constructed for mission services. The Wesleyan Mission accordingly obtained possession, and at once adapted them for its purposes. A second and very valuable lodgment has thus been effected in this district, and campaigning agencies are carried on here as at the Bar. In both cases a restaurant on the premises keeps the mission in further touch with the people.

The two chief citadels of the mission whose outposts we have thus described have now to be noticed. These are Stepney Temple, in the Commercial Road ; and St. George's Chapel, Cable Street. Both are old established Wesleyan Chapels, very large, spacious, and impressive-looking buildings, being indeed survivals of older and more prosperous East London ; and both have been made over, during the last ten years, to the permanent work of the East End Mission.

At St. George's Wesleyan Chapel, Cable Street, the Sunday visitor will find himself in a very large, old-time sanctuary, situate close to Ratcliff Highway.

The more settled Wesleyan congregation is to be seen in the morning ; but in the evening, specially in the winter months, the mission character of the service is attested by a more miscellaneous audience. They are chiefly outsiders, numbering some seven or eight hundred persons. This is an extremely large congregation for such a district. Often at the week evening service as many as a thousand persons are present.

There are also Sunday schools, not only for children, of whom some five hundred are in attendance, but for men and for women, the last-named being specially a means and result of mission work. In the afternoon, the girls' parlour is the scene of some very interesting work among the roughest working-girls of the locality. These, in many cases, are brought in from courts and alleys where the conditions of life were previously against them.

The children's mission is another admirable agency. It gathers in troops of little ones who have been hitherto outside Sunday-school or even ragged-school influences. Twice a week

ST. GEORGE'S WESLEYAN CHAPEL.

the children gather in the schoolrooms in hundreds. In addition, there are five hundred children of a less neglected class attending the Sunday schools.

Not the least important part of the mission is the Sunday outdoor work, including the recruiting service in the open air, which enlists converts into the ranks, and leads to their regularly attending headquarters at Cable Street.

The Commercial Road centre of the mission is Stepney Temple, formerly the Seamen's Chapel Street. It is within easy touch of its colleague in St. George's, Cable Street. The two are near enough to each other to admit of united action upon a given spot, whether the scene be Commercial Road or Ratcliff Highway. Under its older name, Stepney Temple had an excellent record of evangelistic services in years when seamen were more numerous in the locality than they are now. The building is a very imposing structure, and is admirably placed for commanding the great thoroughfare.

A visit on Sunday impresses us in many ways. The roomy and lofty interior is beautifully decorated, and the deep galleries and spacious floor accommodate fully twelve hundred people. Properly to see and appreciate the newer uses of Stepney Temple, the visit should be paid on a winter Sunday or week-day evening, when it is often completely filled. The service throughout is inspired by the truly Wesleyan zeal and enthusiasm which the Rev. Peter Thompson and his colleagues, Mr. Howard and Mr. Jackson and their lay helpers, have brought to their work. An orchestral band and a well-trained choir lead the musical part of the service.

A visit to the Lycett Memorial Chapel in the Mile End Road, and to the mission centre at Crowder Street, Wapping, would amply confirm the impression that in its great forward movement in the East of London, Wesleyan Methodism is nobly maintaining its time-honoured methods and its consecrated zeal for the evangelisation of the people.

Two important Homes for sailors in Ratcliff Highway have yet to be mentioned. Sailors all round the world are now getting to know The Welcome Home, at 173 St. George Street, where Miss Child has for many years proved herself the seamen's hospitable and devoted friend and evangelist. The Home provides comfortable and cheap lodgings, where the sailor's clothes and money are in safe keeping. There are free suppers and lodgings for helping the destitute to tide over until they can ship again. There is a book-bag mission for supplying each sailor as he reaches the port with a bag of good wholesome literature; and lastly, the Home is the headquarters of the Christian Lifeboat Crew, which has branches in most of the great seaports of the world.

A Sunday evening service in the 'foc'sle' of the Welcome Home reveals one of the cheeriest and most effective of the agencies which are reforming Ratcliff Highway. The harmonium for the service was subscribed and presented to the Home by the sailors frequenting the place, as a token of their gratitude. To know the full scope of the mission, a visit on another day than Sunday would be necessary.

To Miss Macpherson and Miss Child, pioneers many years since in this and other good works in the Highway, the district is indebted much more than it knows.

At the corner of Betts Street we shall find another evangelical mission and house of call for sailors, known far and wide as The Sailors' Rest. Established some eighteen years since, its Sunday and week-day agencies among sailors far from home have made it well known amongst seamen coming to the port and London, who here get practical help and guidance of much value to strangers in the great city. The Sunday-night meetings are much prized, and one of the results of these gatherings is seen in the training of converts for mission work. During one year, some fifteen hundred meetings have been held, and addresses given in English, Swedish, German, French, Italian, Spanish, Portuguese, and Lettish.[1]

At Old Gravel Lane, which runs from Ratcliff Highway across the 'Bridge of Sighs' through the London Docks to Wapping, we enter the parish of St. Peter's in the East. St. Peter's, London Docks, as it is more generally called, is memorable in the annals of East London as the scene of the work of the Rev. Charles Lowder, who, with untold labours and an heroic self-devotion, spent twenty-three years in mission work amongst the most degraded of East London, and died a premature death from exhaustion and anxiety.

The story is still fresh in the hearts of the people for whom he

[1] The Honorary Secretary is Mr. J. Theo. Isaacs, 163 St. George's Street, E.

spent himself. As we stand on the ominous drawbridge in Old
Gravel Lane, the last resort of so many ruined lives, we hear
afresh from one of Mr. Lowder's flock the story of the district as
it was in 1856.

Mr. Lowder came here as a young man fresh from Oxford.
It was here that 'he heard a cry of mingled agony, suffering,
laughter, and blasphemy coming from these depths, that rang in
his ears, go where he would.' The difficulties of the work to
which he set himself were enormous. Thirty thousand souls
were here in one parish, but the clergyman had never ventured
out of the church to teach. It was this neglected outdoor work
to which the new-comer devoted himself, and with which his
name is chiefly associated. He founded a church in the heart of
the district, as well as a number of mission agencies almost as
numerous as the needs of the people.

'The pastoral kindness and genuine piety of Lowder,' writes
the Rev. Harry Jones, who knew him well, 'gradually wore off
the edge of the bitter animosity felt towards his ceremonialism,
and he was buried amid the tears of his flock. The half-savage
denizens of the lowest part of St. George's and Wapping, who
had once attacked him and tried to throw him over the
drawbridge, had learned to respect a man whom they had seen
stopping many a street fight, or facing an infuriated mob, or
ministering to the bodily and spiritual wants of the victims to
Asiatic cholera, sometimes carrying the sufferers in his arms to
the hospital.'

St. Peter's Church and clergy-house form a substantial and
striking group of buildings in such a district. The church seats
five hundred. On Sunday morning we find a respectably
dressed congregation of two or three hundred, and at night a
full church. There is a Sunday school of three hundred and
thirty, and a day school of seven hundred. Mr. Wainwright
(Mr. Lowder's successor) follows in the footsteps of his
forerunner. There are some thirty guilds, confraternities,
clubs, *crèches*, and 'socials' of all kinds kept at work under the
superintendence of the vicar and his five assistant clergy. The
work is extremely arduous, and there is still much poverty

among a class belonging to that residuum of humanity which apparently only a maritime city can show.

But the general aspect of the place has been changed immensely for the better concurrently with and subsequent to Mr. Lowder's beneficent work. Rebuilding has been carried on upon a great scale; a beautiful recreation ground has been opened on the Wapping side, on the site of a condemned area of three acres; and one of the greatest of Board schools has been opened in Old Gravel Lane. It should be said that Mr. Lowder's work for the London Docks gave a fresh impetus for the establishment of the University Missions in East London. It has certainly provided a very different Sunday from that which was familiar to visitors to the place some thirty years since.

One of the latest developments of East London mission work is to be seen in Eastern Ratcliff. This is the Shelter at Medland Hall, Medland Street, near the Limehouse Basin. The mission is one of several which have been established by the London Congregationalists, and it attempts to deal socially and religiously with men who are homeless and destitute. A visit to the Hall on Sunday evening will acquaint us with the nature and scope of the work, and at the same time with a religious service almost unique in its character.

Here again the approaches are streets in which the one-room families of the industrial poor are camping out in the open air this warm summer evening. We shall hardly expect to find the Medland Hall service well attended at a time when all Sunday evening congregations are diminished by the outdoor attractions and fine weather. Medland Hall is at the end of a narrow street—a good substantial building externally, and in better days a Congregational chapel.

The scene within is an imposing sight. In spite of the heat, the building is filled with some five hundred men. It is a congregation of casuals. Many of the men have no coats, and are sitting in their shirt-sleeves. On the platform, with the speakers, are several helpers of both sexes, who are trained and accomplished singers, and they accompany on the piano, or speak to the audience.

Seated at the piano as we entered was one of the men from the audience ; he was singing and playing the solo verse of the hymn, the whole of the audience joining their comrade with a will in the chorus. Very soon the plan of a novel and remarkably impressive service was revealed.

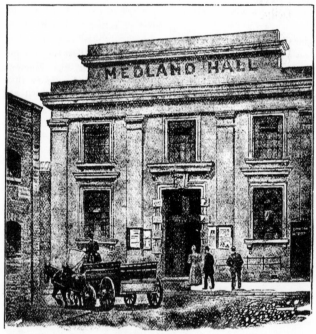

MEDLAND HALL.

The service is chiefly a 'song service.' The gospel is proclaimed by song and story. Long addresses are carefully avoided. 'Experience has convinced me,' says Mr. Wilson Gates, the founder and conductor of these services, 'that the power of the masses to listen continuously, and follow a speaker consecutively through a carefully planned address, is very much overrated. Such addresses, varying in length from fifteen minutes to fifty, are doubtless spiritual meat to vast numbers of Christian people who have been used from their infancy to attend a place of worship, and to follow the preacher ; but here we have to meet with a very different state of things. Song-sermons, followed up by three minutes of pointed application of the words to personal needs, have somehow got a firmer hold on the ears and hearts of the homeless men who meet together at Medland Hall.'

The service is begun with two of Sankey's hymns. A portion of Scripture is read, and then all unite in the General Confession. This is followed by the Lord's Prayer. Then the 'song service' proper is entered upon. The words of the hymns, which are especially appropriate to the audience, are printed in bold letters on a sheet hung up over the platform, and easily legible in all parts of the hall. As we sit upon the platform it is touching to hear some five hundred homeless men singing to the familiar tune of ' Auld Lang Syne' the following verses :—

> The foxes had their hiding-place,
>   The birds their nightly bed ;
> But Jesus had not anywhere
>   To lay His weary head.
>
> *Should Christ, our Friend, be e'er forgot,*
>   *Or never brought to mind ;*
> *We'll sing His love and kindness yet,*
>   *As in days of Auld Lang Syne.*
>
> He went about from place to place,
>   And had no settled home ;
> He slept in boats, or on the hills,
>   Where'er He chanced to roam.
>
> He is the Friend of homeless men,
>   He knows them young and old ;
> And longs to shelter every one
>   Within His blessèd fold.
>
> Where'er we go this Friend is near,
>   The Friend who for us died ;
> And if our hearts but welcome Him,
>   He'll aye with us abide.'

These simple and homely words, which were sung from the heart, are powerfully felt where more refined hymn-writing would fail. In a gathering of so social and informal a kind, the more domestic compositions naturally find a place. 'The Better Land' and 'The Lighthouse' were among the solos sung from the platform, and, it may be added, heartily applauded by the audience, whose demonstrations and pleasure often find utterance during the evening, and who appreciate the very competent service kindly rendered to them in this form by volunteers who come every Sunday night from a considerable distance to serve them.

Novel as the service may be, and largely as it is entrusted to the men themselves, it is never allowed to get out of hand. The three-minute sermons are heart-searching and affectionate. A strong personal hold on the men is established, and reformations in life and character abundantly attest the value of the mission.

Of the way in which the spiritual work is followed up, and of the large number of men who are restored to honest and success-ful industry, this is not the occasion to tell; but it may be said that many men who starve in the glutted labour market in East London are migrated to guaranteed employment in the colonies, and that in the first five months of the present year fifty-two were sent to situations in Canada.

'Medland Hall,' says our guide, Mr. Gates, 'is not only a place of worship; it is a shelter and a restaurant. Foot-sore and heart-sore, men here find shelter and refreshment night after night. The solid food given to the poor fellows only costs a halfpenny each man per night. Religious services which com-mence with bread and butter and coffee may not be conventional, but they are very much appreciated by hungry men. Such an introduction gives a new meaning to the beatitudes which follow, and the realisation of rest for the body affords a telling illustra-tion of Christ's invitation to the weary of heart.'

It is impossible to conclude a brief survey of a district abounding in Christian workers amid scenes of poverty and sorrow, sin and misery, without a word of reference to Miss Steer's 'Bridge of Hope' in Betts Street. Although the work carried on at this 'home of penitence and industry' may not come within the scope of observation of the Sunday visitor, it

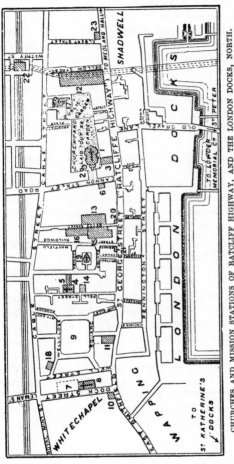

CHURCHES AND MISSION STATIONS OF RATCLIFF HIGHWAY, AND THE LONDON DOCKS, NORTH.

1. Parish Church.
2. Rectory House and Parish Room.
3. St. George's Mission House.
4. St. Matthew's Church & Mission Room.
5. Church Army Labour Home.
6. Girls' Friendly Lodge.
7. Sailors' Home.
8. St. Paul's, Dock Street.

9. St. Paul's Mission School.
10. Church Extension Mission and Restaurant.
11. Seamen's Christian Friend Society.
12. Highway Board School.
13. Betts Street Board School.
14. Roman Catholic Infant School.
15. Public Baths and Wash-House.

16. Miss Steer's Highway Refuge.
17. St. George's Wesleyan Chapel.
18. Old Mahogany Bar.
19. Swedish Church.
20. The Stranger's Rest.
21. Sailor's Welcome Home.
22. Shadwell Station.
23. Paddy's Goose.

179

has too intimate a relationship to the mission needs of Ratcliff to be altogether ignored in these sketches.

It is eleven years since Miss Steer was enabled to take three houses—one of them a drinking and dancing saloon in the notorious Betts Street—and turn them into a refuge. To-day the spacious dancing-room in the rear is a pretty and bright little mission hall.

'We live down here,' says Miss Steer, 'to help the women and children around us.' The agencies are a refuge, a night shelter, and cottage homes in the country for children.

'One of the most painfully interesting branches at the beginning of the work,' continued Miss Steer, 'was the classes held for children out of the bad houses. It was easy enough to gather such a class then; to-day it would be absolutely impossible. The effectual working of the Industrial Schools Amendment Act, and later on the Criminal Law Amendment Bill, have made a marvellous change. In many other ways St. George's in the East has changed since 1879 for the better.

'Betts Street, when first I knew it, contained thirty-five houses of the worst repute; now it is one of the most respectable streets in the locality; and in it stands our beautiful Refuge, a visible sign of what the power of God can do.

But if the Ratcliff Highway of to-day compares favourably with that of the past, its problems still perplex the judgment. The more hideous side of human life appeals with a greater intensity and pathos the more it is known. It is from this point of view that Miss Steer lately wrote: 'I have realised more than ever before the enormous force of the powers of evil against us. Sin in all its hideousness lifts its hydra head at every turn, and the difficulties seem overwhelming. Yet in the larger view we see that "the Lord reigneth." All pioneer work is rough and difficult; but are there ever any times more blessed to look back upon?'

Those who know Ratcliff Highway best are the most appreciative of Miss Steer's work. It is pleasant to find among her near friends and co-workers the names of the present rector of St. George's and his predecessor, the Rev. Harry Jones, as well as the Rev. Peter Thompson, of the Wesleyan Mission.

XII

VICTORIA PARK

NLY a great world metropolis and seaport can show such strange and moving pictures, such startling lights and shadows, as those which startle the stranger to East London. In these our Sunday visits to the populous region of labour and poverty, we have had glimpses of the life of the people in the eastern City's highways and byways; in the Ghetto and the synagogue; the churches, chapels, and mission halls; in lodging-houses, night-shelters, and open-air markets; among the shipping docks and by the waterside.

And yet our gallery of East London's living pictures is far from complete, and many features of the Sunday life of the million-peopled city remain unrecorded. One of the most important of these is the outdoor life of East London, as seen in the great holiday gathering-ground, Victoria Park. It will be found to throw considerable light upon traits of East End character and tendencies not seen on so great a scale elsewhere.

Victoria Park on the Sunday is one of the great revelations and surprises of East London. As a vast open-air resort and breathing-place it is admirably situated. The regions of Eastern Bethnal Green and the Mile End Road, with their thousands of storied tenements, teeming with an industrious population, are within easy reach of its beautiful lakes, its luxurious foliage, and its spacious greensward. Its hundreds of acres of varied scenery, well wooded and watered, with open spaces for great concourses of holiday-seekers, make it the chief ornament and pride of East London for outdoor purposes.

We make our way to the head of the beautiful lakes near the grand drinking fountain erected by Lady Burdett Coutts. It towers aloft as a beautiful beacon amid the trees. Here, by common consent, is the goal of the multitude. Under the shade of the fine clumps of spreading trees and in the open spaces around is the great East End arena in which some thousands assemble for talk and discussion every Sunday afternoon.

For, strange as it may seem, the chief attraction of Victoria Park on Sundays is not the beautiful scenery or the pure and almost country air. The enjoyment of the populace is of quite another kind. In the eyes of Bethnal Green and Mile End, the delights of public controversy and debate eclipse every other pleasure which the Park can offer.

On the open greensward, or beneath the shades of the elms and willows, are massed, in separate crowds, thousands of working-men. Here they stand for hours to uphold and applaud their favourite controversialist, or to give a hearing to some new propaganda in politics and religion. A few may be drawn hither by idle curiosity ; but as a whole the crowds are keenly interested in the subjects of dispute, and range themselves on the one side or the other.

This extremely pretty region of Victoria Park is in fact black with crowds of men of all ages. Women, with the exception of one of the gatherings, are almost entirely absent. Each company gathers around its own spokesman, or listens to a rival who in turn ascends the rostrum to exercise the right of reply. Altogether there are often a dozen large crowds assembled here on Sunday afternoons, some of them numbering a thousand persons.

Let us make the tour of the ground, calling in upon each group, and prepared to learn something of the inner life and thoughts of the working classes of East London.

The National Secularist Society, with banner and portable tribune, is here in considerable force. Sunday after Sunday, its clever and practised speakers hardly ever fail to hold a large audience. The Roman Catholics, too, are ably represented by

VICTORIA PARK.

their most active and indefatigable open-air propagandists, the well-known 'Ransomers,' members of the Guild of Our Lady of Ransom. They are opposed by a band of the Protestant Alliance. Politics are represented by the Social Democratic Federation and the Independent Labour Party, but their following is not large as compared with the crowds who are interested in religious discussion.

Almost at the entrance to the forum, and under the well-known group of trees known as 'The Eight Sisters,' is assembled the Tower Hamlets Mission, from the Great Assembly Hall in the Mile End Road. We heard the strains of their splendid brass band floating over the trees as we entered the Park. Their audience is always large, although, as we shall see, the proceedings are not controversial. Here, and here only, many women form part of the audience.

Lastly, but perhaps first of all in numbers and importance, is the meeting held by the Christian Evidence Society. Here we shall find as the chief speaker the well-known and highly popular Principal of Oxford House, the Rev. F. Winnington Ingram, who resides hard by, in the famous University Settlement at Bethnal Green.

Such are some of the chief representatives of East London intellectual and religious life to be found in Victoria Park on Sunday afternoon. Occasionally, the Theosophists from Mile End and Bow contend for a hearing, but with very little encouragement.

With one exception, that of a young man who is reciting burlesque melodrama to a couple of hundred of boys and girls, there is no attempt to provide amusement. All are engaged in strenuous controversy on social questions, as seen from the religious, political, or economic point of view.

At first sight there is much to perplex and sadden the visitor, as he moves about in this Babel of disputants. In the Secularist crowd more especially, we hear men as of old 'contradicting and blaspheming.' The number of young men, 'busy mockers' of extreme Socialistic opinions, who are haranguing their hearers from this point of view, are an unpleasant feature of the scene.

But as regards the multitude as a whole, we shall find much to brighten the picture. It is soon obvious that the atheistic party are by no means in the ascendant, and that an antidote of considerable value is at hand to counteract their teaching.

This antidote is supplied by the great meetings of the Christian Evidence Society on the one hand and the earnest

OXFORD HOUSE
UNIVERSITY SETTLEMENT

evangelical and uncontroversial service of praise, testimony, and exhortation from the Tower Hamlets Mission on the other. Let us join the first-named of these groups, the Christian Evidence Society, and learn something of the methods and views of the speakers.

We take our place on the greensward among the thousand people or more who form the Christian Evidence audience. The lecturer, Principal Ingram, ascends the rostrum to open the proceedings. An inscription on the lectern tells us that this East London Branch of the Christian Evidence Society was established by the late Mr. Celestine Edwards, the well-known Victoria Park lecturer, a man of colour and of great ability, whose death closed a most useful evangelistic life.

Cordially welcomed by the crowd, Principal Ingram announces to strangers that he is not there to conduct a religious service, but solely to speak on questions in which his friends the working-men are interested, and to deal with any controversial or other questions from opponents.

The lecture then follows. The subject at these meetings is usually one on which the opponents themselves have challenged discussion. To-day the question for consideration and debate is, ' What has Christianity done for the Working Classes ? ' The theme is a favourite one with the Victoria Park Secularist. On previous Sundays it has been preceded by the subject, ' Is there a God ? ' ' What has God done for me ? ' ' Old Testament Difficulties,' and ' New Testament Morality.' The Christian Evidence Society prefers that opponents should select their own questions, and thus reveal the subjects which are chiefly put forward among working-men as obstacles to Christianity.

As the lecturer proceeds, a stranger to Victoria Park would be struck with the remarkably high level upon which the subject is treated, the intelligence it presumes on the part of the audience, and the careful courtesy it shows towards opponents.

In an address of an hour's duration, delivered in a most engaging manner, and varied with admirably good-tempered replies to a few interruptions, the speaker establishes his case by means of the historical evidence. He shows that the working-man owes his weekly day of rest to Christianity ; that Christianity has abolished slavery and personal servitude ; has given him a home of his own, and the weekly wages of a free man. The references to church history, civic history, and economic history, are carefully and explicitly given.

The speaker gets an excellent hearing from the great audience, who follow him with unbroken attention. Interruptions are very few, and mostly from strangers, unused to the courtesies which have been gradually established at these meetings. At the close the lecturer descends from the rostrum and gives place to an opponent, who endeavours to answer or contravene the lecturer's arguments. He also obtains a fair hearing.

The lecturer then replies. The interest of the audience is intense, and demonstrations are frequent. A storm of rain may come on, but the meeting is unaffected, and the lecturer carries his argument to its conclusion. In his final words, Principal Ingram urges with earnestness and affection the claim which Christ has established on working-men, whose trials He has known and shared, and who, he tells them, 'is not far from every one of you.'

The announcements for the following Sunday having been made, Principal Ingram takes a friendly leave of the meeting and of his opponents. Crowds follow him as he goes, eager to press the hand of one who knows them well, treats them tenderly, and always gives the answer which turns away wrath.

It is right to add that these meetings under the auspices of the Christian Evidence Society are not simply controversial. On this particular occasion, it is gratifying to learn that a collection made at the previous meeting on behalf of the Sunday Hospital Fund amounted to forty pounds.

Christian controversialists generally may be interested to know that Mr. Ingram spares no pains to equip himself for his difficult work. As a rule, many in his audience are extremely well read in the sceptical literature of the day and in the later Biblical criticism, especially as set forth in the favourite weekly journal of the Secularists, *The Freethinker*. His own opinion of the work to which he devotes his Sundays, and of those for whom he labours, is valuable, and will throw some light upon what has been already said.

'I may be asked,' said Mr. Ingram, 'why I attach so much importance to these open-air efforts of ours to deal with working-men. An objector might say, "Are there no church services, no mission services, no house-to-house visiting, no city missionaries and others for the defence and confirmation of the gospel?"

'Well, my answer to that is that we must look to the habits of East End working-men, and take them as we find them. They remind me of the ancient Athenians. They have a passion for outdoor discussion. Anywhere in East London you can draw a crowd in three minutes. Whether or not you can hold them is another matter.

'There is a good reason for the method we adopt in Victoria Park. We might, if we chose, go from one crowd to another, waiting for a chance of answering a Secularist lecturer, as I once did ; but I have found it very much better to have a stand of my own. I can thus take my time fairly to state my subject and work it out, rather than spend my breath in trying to answer in a short ten minutes a long hour's lecture by some-body else. Not that you will be discourteously treated at the other stand. All controversialists should remember that "with what measure ye mete, it will be measured to you again"; but it is really a question of economy of time, and it is obviously better for you to have the hour than the ten minutes, even if you are courteously given double time.

'What is wanted,' continued Principal Ingram, 'in these out-door meetings, and what I endeavour to supply, is definite teaching of facts, carefully substantiated and illustrated, as an antidote to the vague and sweeping negative statements which are so common on the other side.

'Of history, the majority are profoundly ignorant, and are therefore at the mercy of almost any statement. Thus, in answer to a description of the state of morality in some eighteen centuries ago, as given by Tacitus and Juvenal, it was replied that "Rome was really quite a moral place eighteen centuries ago, and was only blackened by the Christians, to throw their religion into a brighter light!" Among the audience of one thousand men, there was not sufficient knowledge to decide what was right.

'All that we hear on the side of Christian evidence from our Lightfoots, Westcotts, and Salmons, is a closed book to them. When I had explained at some length, one Sunday afternoon, that many New Testament difficulties arise from mistranslations or misunderstanding of the original Greek text, such as in the case of " Woman, what have I to do with thee ?" " Take no thought for the morrow," etc., the only reply was this : " Do you really suppose that if the Christian religion had been meant for the world, *its documents would have been written in Greek* ?" '

Here we ventured to remind Principal Ingram of his statement that Secularists find the most promising ground for their teaching in the working class of our great cities. How was that to be explained ?

'There are several reasons,' Mr. Ingram replied. ' In the first place, working-men see more of the suffering of the world than other people. The prosperous merchant, or well-to-do tradesman, finds the world fairly comfortable as it is ; he often considers it the best of all possible worlds. But the working-man sees the other side ; by far the most effective speeches made by Secularists in Victoria Park, and the hardest to answer, are those which harp upon the theme that God either cannot cure the misery there is in the world, or that He does not care to do so ; these are the only speeches which, as a rule, carry the audience away.

' But with most of the questions on which we are challenged, we must not take the objector too seriously, although we must try to meet his argument. His scepticism is only skin-deep, and with a change of temper and attitude towards Christianity—best of all a change of heart—his animosity disappears. We need the grace of Christ Himself in dealing with them, and after many years of work amongst them I can gratefully say that the prospects are most encouraging. Many of the Secularists themselves, I am bound to say, especially in East London, are honest and kind-hearted men, and some are personal friends of mine. I have always received the most courteous reception at their stand in the Park, and have sometimes been given double time to reply.'

Let us now take a look at the closing scenes in the Park as the groups are beginning to disperse to their homes. The Babel of voices of which we have spoken has ceased. The Mission Corps from the Tower Hamlets are closing their service of prayer, exhortation, and praise beneath the full-foliaged trees. As we wait, with the echoes of controversy still in our ears, it is touching to hear them sing their favourite hymn of appeal to the passing multitude—

'Jesus calls us o'er the tumult!'

Many are the willing listeners, who come from the dissolving crowds around. Not less appropriate and impressive than the words we have just heard is the final hymn, addressed to weary doubters—

'I heard the voice of Jesus say,
  "Behold, I freely give
The living water; thirsty one,
  Stoop down, and drink, and live!"
I came to Jesus, and I drank
  Of that life-giving stream;
My thirst was quenched, my soul revived,
  And now I live in Him.'

Such is the testimony of not a few who labour in Victoria Park Sunday after Sunday for the salvation and happiness of their fellow-men.

But the time has now come for our memoirs of Sunday in East London to be brought to a close. A contribution, and nothing more, to an almost boundless subject is all that has been attempted. Many are the aspects of human need and Christian work in England's great imperial city which must be left unrecorded. Among the devoted workers for the most neglected classes of East London, the Roman Catholics have a prominent place. They carry out with much self-sacrifice their own ideals of service to the very poor. The Salvation Army, too, perhaps less numerous in East London than might have been expected, are yet doing a noble work for the vicious and the wretched. At Dr. Barnardo's great mission centre in Limehouse, The Edinburgh Castle, we should find assembled on the Sunday evening a congregation of more than four thousand people, and should learn much of the influence of evangelical religion in a poor and populous region but little known to Londoners at large. Mansfield House in Canning Town, established on the basis of the University Settlements in East London, was described in *The Leisure Hour* for July 1895 (p. 600).

Such are some of the agencies which would further swell the record of the East London Sunday. But we must leave them with little more than the bare mention of their names. Yet how much deeper and intenser a sympathy with all that is

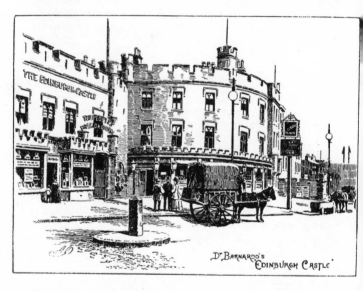

Dr BARNARDO'S EDINBURGH CASTLE

Christ-like and humane in their work, and indeed with all true yokefellows and fellow-labourers in the same hallowed and happy service, is born of one single year of Sundays spent in the highways and byways of East London!